Good Courts

GOOD COURTS

The Case for Problem-Solving Justice

GREG BERMAN AND JOHN FEINBLATT

with Sarah Glazer

THE NEW PRESS

NEW YORK
LONDON

The opinions expressed in this book do not necessarily
represent the official positions of the City of New York
or the New York State Court system.

Published in the United States by The New Press, New York, 2005
Distributed by W. W. Norton & Company, Inc., New York

LIBRARY OF CONGRESS CATALOGING-IN-PUBLICATION DATA

Berman, Greg.
    Good courts: the case for problem-solving justice / Greg Berman
    and John Feinblatt; with Sarah Glazer.
        p. cm.
    Includes bibliographical references and index.
    ISBN 1-56584-973-6 (hardbound)
1. Criminal courts—United States. 2. Drug courts—United States.
3. Domestic relations courts—United States. 4. Neighborhood justice centers—
United States. 5. Criminal justice, Administration of—United States.
6. Problem solving—United States. I. Feinblatt, John. II. Glazer, Sarah.
III. Title

KF9223.B47 2004
345.73'01—dc22   2004063176

The New Press was established in 1990 as a not-for-profit
alternative to the large, commercial publishing houses currently
dominating the book publishing industry. The New Press operates
in the public interest rather than for private gain, and is committed
to publishing, in innovative ways, works of educational, cultural,
and community value that are often deemed insufficiently profitable.

www.thenewpress.com

Book design and composition by Hall Smyth

Printed in the United States of America

10 9 8 7 6 5 4 3 2 1

DEDICATION

To Hon. Judith S. Kaye and Hon. Jonathan Lippman
for their vision, leadership, and counsel

Contents

Acknowledgments

One of the secret pleasures of reading any book is lingering over the acknowledgments, which often offer a glimpse of the behind-the-scenes story of how a book was actually written. It would be nice to pretend that this book emerged *sui generis*, but the truth is that it is the product of dozens of people—friends, colleagues, funders, and others.

First and foremost, this book would not have been possible without New York State Chief Judge Judith S. Kaye and Chief Administrative Judge Jonathan Lippman. They have been the most visible public champions of not only problem-solving justice but the Center for Court Innovation as well. We owe them a debt that we will probably never be able to repay fully. We also thank New York City Mayor Michael R. Bloomberg. Under his leadership, New York City continues to be a testing ground for problem-solving justice.

Thanks as well to Diane Wachtell at The New Press for her willingness to take a chance on a couple of first-time authors; to David Anderson of the Ford Foundation for connecting us to Diane; to Mary McCormick of the Fund for the City of New York for providing us with an institutional home; to Herb Sturz, Gerald Schoenfeld, and Gretchen Dykstra for giving us the opportunity to experiment with problem-solving courts in the first place, and to Andrew Kimball for facilitating our access to the Allen Room at the New York Public Library, which offered us space to write and room to breathe.

Special thanks to freelance journalist Sarah Glazer for helping us make the crucial move from talking about a book to actually writing one. Sarah's contributions can be found throughout this book, especially in chapters 3 and 5, which rely heavily on her solid reporting and clear prose. Equally important, Sarah's persistent questioning pushed us to refine our thinking and sharpen our language about problem-solving justice. For this, we are extremely grateful.

The principal funders who underwrote our work on this book were the William and Flora Hewlett Foundation, the State Justice Institute, and an anonymous donor-advised fund at Rockefeller Philanthropy Advisors. Special thanks to Paul Brest, Dave Tevelin, Penny Fujiko Willgerodt, and Barbra Mazur for making this possible.

A number of past and present staff people at the Center for Court Innovation have contributed to this book—offering ideas, conducting interviews, and providing support, both administrative and moral. We have attempted to highlight their specific contributions throughout the manuscript, but it is worth offering blanket thanks as well to Robert Wolf, Anne Gulick, Aubrey Fox, Michael Rempel, Nora Puffett, Derek Denckla, Robert Feldstein, Liz Glazer, Sharon Bryant, Veronica Ramadan, Julius Lang, Valerie Raine, Raye Barbieri, Carol Fisler, Jason Chopoorian, Amy Levitt, Amanda Burden, Emily Sack, Michele Sviridoff, Liberty Aldrich, Adam Mansky, Al Siegel, and Eric Lee.

Thanks as well to all of the judges, attorneys, and administrators from problem-solving courts who appear in this book. It is their hard work on the ground that fills these pages. We hope we have accurately conveyed the courage and dedication they bring to their work. Special thanks to judges Robert G.M. Keating and Judy Harris Kluger for their pioneering efforts, and to Alex Calabrese, the presiding judge of the Red Hook Community Justice Center, who reviewed earlier versions of this manuscript.

Finally, we would like to thank our families—Jonathan, Maeve, Michele, Allan, M.J., Carolyn, Hannah, and Milly—for their love, patience, and encouragement.

Good Courts

INTRODUCTION

A New Approach to Justice

This book is about a quiet revolution among American criminal courts. In some respects, the fact that change is happening within the judicial branch should come as little surprise. After all, no civic institution has experienced a greater loss of public faith in recent years, even in the face of historic reductions in crime in many parts of the country. Public opinion polls consistently reveal frustration with "revolving-door justice"—the perception that criminal courts recycle offenders through the system. The list of complaints is long: courts are too slow, judges are out of touch, the needs of victims are ignored, and offenders continue to commit the same crimes again and again.

In response, an innovative group of judges and attorneys has begun to test new ways of doing justice, reengineering how courts address such everyday problems as quality-of-life crime, drugs, and domestic violence. These innovators are united by the common belief that courts need to reassert their relevance in society and that judges and attorneys have an obligation to address the problems that bring people to court, whether as victims, defendants, or simply concerned citizens.

This book is an attempt to describe the history, objectives, and achievements of a national movement toward "problem-solving justice" that, in just a little more than a decade, has moved from a handful of isolated projects to the brink of achieving real and lasting change within the judiciary.

For too long, American courts have taken a one-size-fits-all approach to criminal cases. No matter what kind of case—murder or misdemeanor—the courts offered the same basic process: an adversarial contest between two advocates moderated by an impartial third party. This system, at least in theory, offers the comfort of uniformity, fairness, and neutrality. And in many cases, the current system works just fine. For murders, rapes, and robberies, it can be argued that the traditional approach does a more-or-less effective job of protecting both public safety and the rights of defendants. But these crimes represent just a tiny fraction of the caseload of state courts, which each year are asked to resolve millions of cases involving minor offenses (such as prostitution, low-level drug possession, and disorderly conduct) that are committed by offenders with a range of serious social problems (including mental illness, addiction, and homelessness). While these cases may be "minor" in a legal sense, they are anything but to the victims and the communities directly affected by crime. And when the same process that works for murderers and rapists is applied to shoplifters, prostitutes, and petty drug offenders, the result, all too often, is the kind of homogenized, assembly-line justice that leaves all parties dissatisfied.

In contrast, hundreds of entrepreneurial, reform-minded judges, attorneys, and administrators working in every state in the nation have come to believe that cases cannot be treated as an undifferentiated mass, regardless of the nature or complexity of the issue at hand. Problem-solving justice is an umbrella term that describes a wide range of specialized courtrooms that are working to ensure not just that the punishment fits the crime (as courts have always tried to do, with varying degrees of success) but that the process fits the problem. These innovative courts encourage judges and attorneys to think of themselves as problem solvers rather than as simply case processors.

For problem-solving judges and attorneys, a case is a problem to be solved, not just a matter to be adjucated. Moreover, instead of seeing each case as an isolated incident, judges and attorneys in problem-solving courts analyze the cases in front of them for patterns and then fashion responses that seek to change the behavior of offenders, enhance the safety of victims, and improve the quality of life in our communities.

Broadly speaking, there are five key elements to the problem-solving reform agenda:

- *A Tailored Approach to Justice.* A problem-solving court disaggregates the criminal caseload, making sure that judicial resources match the special needs of each case. This is not unlike the "small is better" movement in education, which seeks to break large schools into smaller, more manageable units with specialized themes. Another analogue is the movement toward problem-oriented policing, which requires police officers to analyze crime patterns and then fashion tailor-made responses instead of simply responding to calls for service.
- *Creative Partnerships.* Problem-solving courts welcome new players into the courthouse. They aggressively reach out to neighborhoods to educate community groups and find new ways for citizens to get involved in the judicial process. They also seek to integrate social services—including drug-treatment providers, job-training programs, victim-support groups, and others—into their standard operating procedures. The idea is to give judges and attorneys access to a broader

range of sentencing options. By mandating offenders to receive drug treatment or mental-health counseling or job training or community service, problem-solving courts seek to reduce the criminal justice system's reliance on incarceration, probation, and dispositions that allow offenders to leave court with no sanction whatsoever for criminal behavior.

- *Informed Decision Making.* Problem-solving courts seek to provide judges and attorneys with more information about the cases in front of them, including psychosocial information about offenders and data about the impact of crimes on particular neighborhoods. Shouldn't district attorneys who prosecute domestic violence cases understand the unique dynamics of intimate abuse? Shouldn't a defense attorney who represents clients with substance-abuse problems know something about pharmacology and the recovery process? And shouldn't judges who hear cases from a particular neighborhood understand the crime patterns and hot spots in that community? Problem-solving courts ensure that they do, providing both continuity in the courtroom and enhanced expertise in the issue at hand, be it domestic violence, addiction, or neighborhood crime.

- *Accountability.* Problem-solving courts make aggressive use of judicial monitoring. Instead of diverting offenders out of the system or giving them a get-out-of-jail-free card, problem-solving judges rigorously supervise offenders' performance in social services and community restitution projects. Requiring regular court appearances by offenders reinforces the importance of complying with court orders. It also sends a message to the rest of the system (police, probation, prosecutors, social-service providers, and others) and to the public at large that the courts mean business.

- *A Focus on Results.* Problem-solving justice asks courts to use data to assess their own effectiveness, moving beyond simply tracking how many cases are handled (and how quickly they are processed) to ask hard questions about the impacts of case processing on victims, offenders, and communities. This includes documenting the safety of victims, the number of offenders who are re-arrested, and local perceptions of neighborhood quality of life.

By one estimate, there are no fewer than eleven different kinds of problem-solving courts.[1] For the purposes of this book, we will focus on the three most well developed examples: community courts, domestic-violence courts, and drug courts.

Community courts are neighborhood-focused courtrooms that attempt to tackle the problems of specific, crime-riddled communities, bringing criminal justice officials and local residents together to improve public safety. Most community courts focus on low-level criminal cases—so-called "quality-of-life" crimes like drug possession, prostitution, and vandalism. Offenders are typically sentenced to a combination of punishment and help, including community service to pay back the neighborhood and social services geared toward preventing them from having to return to court again. At the same time, community courts reach out aggressively to local residents, community groups, and businesses, asking them to play a number of roles, including sitting on advisory boards, identifying community-service projects, and meeting face-to-face with offenders to explain the impact of chronic low-level offending.

While community courts typically handle minor criminal cases, domestic-violence courts exclusively handle serious cases involving intimate abuse, a problem that for centuries received scant (and some would say hostile) attention from the criminal justice system. Here, the goal is to provide victims with extensive services—counseling, shelter, advocacy—aimed at preventing further abuse at the hands of their batterers. At the same time, domestic-violence courts strengthen the supervision of defendants, requiring them to participate in batterers' intervention programs and to report to the judge about their compliance with restraining orders while a case is pending.

The most popular brand of problem-solving court is undoubtedly the drug court. Drug courts seek to help addicted offenders achieve sobriety by mandating community-based drug treatment as an alternative to incarceration. Eligibility criteria are established by the judge, prosecutor, and defense attorney. Typically, participants must be addicted (as opposed to recreational users), nonviolent, and must voluntarily agree to a formal plan that details both the length of treatment and the consequences for failure. In most cases, successful participants can avoid jail time by completing treatment. The drug-court judge, who receives special training in how to respond effectively to relapse, establishes accountability by requiring frequent reports and drug tests.

While drug courts, domestic-violence courts, and community courts have received the lion's share of attention to date, they represent just the tip of the iceberg; other problem-solving courts currently being tested include mental-health courts, reentry courts, juvenile drug courts, DWI courts, family-treatment courts, homeless courts, and youth courts.

What does a problem-solving court look like in practice? Take a typical case involving an offender convicted of felony possession of drugs. In most such cases, the offender is not a big-time dealer with a violent history, but rather a hard-core, nonviolent addict caught feeding his habit. How should the courts respond? Many judges are coming to realize that none of the standard choices at their disposal—jail, probation, or dismissal—truly offers a viable, long-term resolution to the case. If you don't tackle the offender's addiction, you haven't really solved the problem—either for the community or for the offender.

In a problem-solving drug court, addressing addiction isn't an afterthought—it's the heart of the matter. After an offender opts into the program, all of the major players in the courtroom—judge, prosecutor, and defense attorney— explicitly acknowledge that the goal is to change his behavior, moving him from addiction to sobriety and from a life of crime to law-abiding behavior.

In pursuit of this goal, the judge uses a broad array of tools, including drug treatment, mental-health counseling, job training, and community-restitution projects. And to ensure accountability, the judge requires offenders to return to court frequently (sometimes weekly)—to report on their progress in treatment, to submit urine tests, and to demonstrate their compliance with court orders. Success in treatment is publicly acknowledged by the judge, sometimes with applause in the courtroom. Graduates typically have the charges against them dropped, while those who fail receive a predetermined jail or prison sentence, no questions asked.

This carrot-and-stick approach has successfully motivated thousands of offenders to get clean and lead productive (and tax-paying) lives. Everybody wins when this happens: the offender because he breaks the cycle of drugs-crime-jail; the court because it no longer has to spend scarce resources on the same offender again and again; and most importantly, the general public wins, because its streets are safer.

Since the opening of the nation's first drug court in Miami-Dade County, Florida, in 1989, problem-solving justice has become an increasingly standard feature of the judicial landscape in the United States. There are now more than 2,000 problem-solving courts.[2] Every state has at least one.

All fifty state-court chief justices have endorsed the further expansion of problem-solving justice, as has the American Bar Association. The interest in problem-solving justice is not confined to the United States. Tony Blair's government has moved to introduce drug courts, community courts, and domestic-violence courts in England and Wales. Problem-solving courts are also being tested or planned in South Africa, Canada, Scotland, New Zealand, Australia, Ireland, Bermuda, Jamaica, and other countries.

Problem-solving courts are not without their critics. Inside the courtroom, problem-solving courts have asked judges and attorneys to alter their behavior in ways both profound and subtle. This includes welcoming new players into the process, monitoring the provision of social services, and focusing the energies of the court on addressing the problems of victims, communities, and defendants. These changes have raised concerns about judicial paternalism, reduced adversarialism, and the appropriate limits of judicial authority.

Outside the courthouse walls, problem-solving courts have asked judges to establish relationships with community groups, to broker relations with government and non-profit agencies, and to think through the real-life impacts of their decisions. As judges have performed this work, they have called into question the independence and neutrality of the judiciary and even the separation-of-powers doctrine.

These concerns—some serious, some minor; some real, some imagined—must be weighed against the tangible benefits of problem-solving courts. Among other things, problem-solving courts have demonstrated the ability to increase judicial access to information, improve the accountability of both offenders and service providers, satisfy communities, and bring new resources into the courthouse. More than this, problem-solving courts have established a solid track record in changing the life trajectories of victims, offenders, and community residents in crime-plagued neighborhoods. Researchers have documented the following results at problem-solving courts across the country[3]:

- *Reduced Substance Abuse:* Research shows that offenders in court-ordered drug treatment succeed at twice the rate of those who seek help voluntarily.
- *Reduced Recidivism:* Graduates of New York drug courts reoffend at a rate that is 71 percent lower than offenders who go through conventional courts.
- *Reductions in Crime:* A study of New York's Midtown Community Court revealed that it helped reduce street prostitution by 56 percent and illegal vending by 24 percent.
- *Increased Accountability:* The Midtown Community Court also improved compliance with community-service sentences by 50 percent.
- *Enhanced Victim Services:* While victim services in conventional courts tend to be a haphazard affair, researchers documented that nearly every victim who appeared in a domestic-violence court in Brooklyn was offered access to shelter, advocacy, and other vital supports. In a study of a domestic-violence court in Tennessee, 76 percent of victims said the court's handling of their case helped them feel safe.
- *Stronger Families:* By helping addicted parents achieve sobriety, drug courts can dramatically shorten the length of time children spend in foster care. A drug court in Manhattan reduced foster-care stays from an average of four years to less than twelve months.
- *Improved Public Confidence in Justice:* Approval ratings for criminal justice agencies have more than doubled in Red Hook, Brooklyn, since the opening of a community court in that neighborhood. Levels of fear have been reduced dramatically.

Despite these kinds of results, there has been surprisingly little reflection about problem-solving innovation to date. With this book, we hope to provide a theoretical and historical framework for problem-solving justice, describing what it is, where it came from, and where it may be headed. Chapter 1 takes a hard look at the current state of American criminal courts. Chapter 2 describes the problem-solving alternative and explores the intellectual foundations of this new movement. Chapter 3 offers a snapshot of several problem-solving courts in action, providing case studies of community courts in Portland, Oregon, and New York City. Chapter 4 takes a look at how problem-solving justice affects the work of judges, with a particular focus on issues of judicial discretion, neutrality, impartiality, and independence. Chapter 5 tells the stories of several individuals who have had their lives changed by problem-solving courts, including a victim and several offenders. Chapters 6 and 7 examine the issues of effectiveness and fairness, detailing the results that problem-solving courts have achieved and the principal criticisms they have generated. We conclude by offering some thoughts about future applications of the problem-solving approach.

Along the way, we make the case that problem solving is not antithetical to the American legal tradition, but rather an embodiment of some of its highest principles. As New York State Chief Judge Judith S. Kaye has written: "Problem-solving courts are courts. They strive to ensure due process, to engage in neutral fact-finding, and to dispense fair and impartial justice. What is different is that these courts have developed a new architecture—including new technology, new staffing and new linkages—to improve the effectiveness of court sanctions like drug treatment and community restitution."[4] Problem-solving courts are simply good courts.

There is little doubt that problem-solving justice will require state courts to make significant investments in research, technology, training, and social-service provision.[5] But the costs of *not* pursuing problem-solving justice are far greater: victims whose needs go unaddressed, offenders who continue to commit crime after crime, and the continued erosion of public trust in justice. Indeed, the evidence suggests than an up-front investment in problem-solving justice reaps significant dividends on the back end—one Oregon study suggests that every dollar spent on drug courts yields ten dollars in cost savings from reduced incarceration, victimization, and crime.[6]

With this in mind, the pages that follow make the case for problem-solving justice, offering a glimpse of what may well turn out to be the future of the American judiciary.

1

Justice in Crisis:
Why Change Is Necessary

*A few years ago, I was working as a judge one night on the
"lobster" shift in Manhattan—a shift that starts at one a.m.
and ends at nine a.m. At about four a.m., a defendant came before
me charged with possession of one glassine of heroin. He had
a conviction record approximately one inch thick with at least
thirty prior arrests for drug possession. The district attorney asked
for thirty days' jail, while the defense attorney asked for ten days'.*

I said, "Why don't we do drug treatment?"

They said, "It's not available."

*I said, "I know there's no treatment at four o'clock in the
morning, but there must be some program where the defendant
can go when the regular court opens."*

They said, "No, there is no treatment available."

*I remember thinking, "What difference does thirty days in jail
or ten days in jail really make? The defendant needs detox and
a long-term residential drug program. Unless that's the sentence,
we might as well reserve his jail bed now for his next stay."
But without treatment as a judicial tool, I sentenced the defendant*

to the thirty days in jail requested by the prosecution.

While that jail sentence resolved the case, resulted in a positive court statistic, helped me dispose of one hundred cases on that shift, and looked efficient, I was frustrated because I knew it was really a failure. A failure for the defendant because he was addicted going into jail and would be addicted coming out; for the community, because the sentence does not address the real issue that brought the defendant to the court and because he was probably committing crimes to support his addiction and would continue this behavior once he was released; and for the court, because the defendant would be coming back again and again, doing life in prison, thirty days at a time.

For serious cases, such as murder, robbery, and rape, the traditional courthouse approach is effective. If the defendant is convicted, a lengthy prison sentence is appropriate, serving to remove the defendant from society. But communities are inundated with low-level crimes that foster the conditions of disorder that destroy quality of life. . . . The traditional courts are poorly equipped to address these problems . . . nothing is being accomplished except pushing papers.

—HON. ALEX CALABRESE, Presiding Judge,
Red Hook Community Justice Center[1]

Walk into any criminal courthouse in any American city. If you're looking for Perry Mason, you'll be gravely disappointed. By and large, today's state courts bear little resemblance to the criminal courts we learn about in civics class or watch on television crime dramas.[2] According to these idealized accounts, courts are insulated from world affairs, concerned only with truth and justice. They take an even-handed approach to the arguments presented by prosecutors and defense counsel, and they patiently gather all the information they need to adjudicate cases fairly and impartially. In this way (so the civics teachers and television script writers tell us) courts pursue a number of important communal goals. They protect individual rights, shielding citizens from the arbitrary use of government power. And they preserve order, making sure our streets are safe and that those who break the law are appropriately punished.

In practice, however, our courts are quite different. Many criminal courts, particularly in urban areas, are crowded, chaotic, and overwhelmed. More disconcertingly, many courts lack a coherent logic. Indeed, judges rarely take a step back to analyze the work they do. If they did, they would see that problems like drugs and mental illness are driving massive increases in the criminal caseload, yet few resources are allocated to address these issues. They would notice that many of the usual criminal justice sanctions—short-term jail, probation, and sentences where the offender is basically told to stay out of trouble—do little to prevent further criminal behavior. They would discover that many attorneys are unhappy in their jobs and don't believe they are making a difference. And they would find that trials—allegedly the bedrock of our legal system—almost never happen.

THE NOT-SO-ADVERSARIAL SYSTEM

The assumption that the adversarial process is the best way to ascertain truth, and therefore justice, is deeply embedded in the American legal system; it goes to the heart of how lawyers are trained and how prosecutors and defense attorneys think of themselves and their profession. Yet despite the Sixth Amendment's promise that "in all criminal prosecutions, the accused shall enjoy the right to a speedy and public trial, by an impartial jury," head-to-head combat before a judge and twelve impartial jurors is exceedingly rare. The O.J. Simpson and Martha Stewart trials may make for good drama, but they have little to do with how most cases are adjudicated in American courts.

Instead of trials, most criminal cases in this country are resolved through negotiation—what is commonly referred to as "plea bargaining." Plea bargaining takes various forms but usually involves the prosecutor and defense attorney striking a deal in which charges and/or punishments are reduced in exchange for a guilty plea, sparing both parties the trouble and expense of a trial. According to the U.S. Department of Justice, in 1998, 94 percent of the felony convictions in state courts were obtained by guilty pleas, while only 6 percent were obtained by trial.[3]

The prevalence of plea bargaining means that instead of doing what they were ostensibly trained to do—try cases—judges, prosecutors, and defense attorneys end up cutting deals for a living. Instead of hosting hard-fought trials where the guilty are punished and the innocent vindicated, our state courts have come to resemble Middle Eastern souks—overcrowded markets where participants engage in highly ritualized negotiations day after day and where the outcomes are basically a foregone conclusion. It is not unusual for prosecutors and defenders to talk about "going rates" for various offenses, as if cases (and defendants) were commodities to be traded. In this marketplace, the emphasis is on quantity and velocity rather than creativity and individualized solutions.

Although there has been an intermittently vigorous debate about the propriety of the practice, plea bargaining has been a staple of American jurisprudence since at least the 1920s.[4] It is more convenient (prosecutors and defend-

ers can dispose of cases more quickly), less risky (prosecutors are guaranteed a guilty verdict and defendants avoid
the potential of a conviction at trial on a more serious
charge), and less resource-intensive (plea negotiations typically help attorneys avoid the months of preparation that
trials require).

Unfortunately, plea bargaining replaces a process that
exalts public participation (jury trial) with a hidden procedure that relies on negotiations between attorneys. It also
fundamentally alters the balance of power in the court system, moving crucial decision-making authority away from
judges and jurors and placing it in the hands of prosecutors.[5] As Columbia University law professor Gerard E. Lynch
explains: "For most defendants, the primary adjudication
they receive is, in fact, an administrative decision by a state
functionary, the prosecutor. . . . The ultimate decision
whether to bring a charge, moreover, or whether to accept
a guilty plea . . . is left to the prosecutor's essentially unre-
viewable choice."[6]

Many within the courts have argued that plea bargaining
is just another word for triage. These judges and lawyers
characterize plea bargaining as a necessary evil, a way to
handle an unmanageable caseload. With literally millions
of new criminal cases each year, state courts must decide
how to allocate their resources—there are simply too many
defendants for everyone to exercise his or her constitutional right to a trial.

Thus the criminal justice system has come to depend
upon plea bargaining. A generation ago, Dorothy Wright
Wilson, the dean of the University of Southern California
Law School, said, "If criminals wanted to grind justice to a
halt, they could do it by banding together and all pleading
not guilty."[7] The same certainly holds true today. According

to former Supreme Court Chief Justice Warren Burger, "The consequence of what might seem on its face a small percentage change in the rate of guilty pleas can be tremendous. A reduction from 90 percent to 80 percent in guilty pleas requires the assignment of twice the judicial manpower and facilities—judges, court reporters, bailiffs, clerks, jurors and courtrooms. A reduction to 70 percent trebles this demand."[8]

The point here is not that state courts should ban plea bargaining—even if they wanted to, they couldn't. Rather, the point is that we should be honest about what really goes on in our courts. If our courts are going to continue to resolve the bulk of cases in this fashion, we need to rethink how we train lawyers, how we design courthouses, and how we explain case processing to victims, community residents, and defendants.

THE TRUTH ABOUT CONSEQUENCES

Over the past several decades, the national conversation about criminal justice has been dominated by "get tough" measures like "three strikes and you're out," "truth in sentencing," and "mandatory minimum" sentencing laws. The resulting growth in America's inmate population (from 500,000 in 1980 to some 2 million in 2001) and prison spending (from $7 billion to $45 billion) has placed an incredible burden on the criminal justice system, forcing decision makers, in more austere fiscal times, to look for new ways to cut costs and reduce the system's reliance on incarceration.[9]

Given the political environment, you might think that everyone found guilty of a crime winds up incarcerated, but the most common sanction for criminal offenders in the United States is, in fact, probation.[10] Probation, the community-based supervision of offenders, isn't a particularly sexy polit-ical issue. Probation departments in many states are the bas-tard stepchildren of the local criminal justice system—under-funded and largely ignored. As a result, the probation system in many parts of the country is on the brink of collapse. In some jurisdictions, caseloads can rise as high as 1,000 per probation officer, making it virtually impossible for most pro-bationers to receive even glancing attention from the officers who are supposedly supervising them.[11] Half of all proba-tioners fail to fulfill the terms of their probation sentences, and in any given year, hundreds of thousands of probationers fail to even report in. Even more disturbing: about two-thirds of all probationers are rearrested for committing a new crime within three years of their original sentence.[12]

While probation is rife with problems, there's something even less effective that's being doled out to thousands of people each year who plead guilty to criminal behavior: no punishment at all. This disposition is often dressed up with more formal-sounding names, like "unconditional dis-charge" or "time served," but it's all the same thing—essen-tially a free ticket out the courthouse door. Robert G.M. Keating, a judge who served for many years on the bench in New York, complained that he had only two options in low-level criminal cases: "Band-Aids or brain surgery." By this he meant that he could either let a misdemeanant off with essentially no sanction or he could throw the offender in jail for a short period, typically less than five days. Neither response seemed to satisfy in a meaningful way any of the four traditional goals of sentencing: specific deterrence (dis-couraging the offender from re-offending), general deter-rence (discouraging others from following suit), rehabilita-tion (helping the offender change his behavior), or retribu-tion (ensuring that the offender gets his "just deserts").

In the early 1990s, as part of the planning process for the Midtown Community Court, researchers from the National Center for State Courts looked at how misdemeanor cases were typically handled at Manhattan's centralized criminal court. The results will not surprise anyone who has spent time in a busy urban courthouse. First, the researchers found that the majority of misdemeanor cases were disposed of by plea bargain at the defendant's first appearance in court at arraignment, meaning that these cases received only the most minimal legal attention and judicial scrutiny.

And what kinds of sanctions did these offenders receive? The research team found that *four out of every ten misdemeanor offenders walked out of criminal court having received no sanction whatsoever for their behavior.* This included offenders sentenced to conditional discharges with no conditions and those sentenced to "time served," where the process of being arrested and arraigned was deemed punishment enough by the court.

Time served is a strange punishment for a number of reasons, not the least of which is that it doesn't differentiate between the innocent and the guilty: even those who are ultimately found not guilty have had to go through the process of being arrested and arraigned. Time-served sentences fail to demonstrate to victims or neighborhoods that the courts take criminal misbehavior seriously. And they do little to prevent an offender from returning to court again in short order. In essence, the courts pass up a golden opportunity to demonstrate to the public that all crime has consequences and to help offenders address their underlying problems (for example, substance abuse) before they fall into the downward spiral of drugs, crime, and ultimately, prison.

Misdemeanors are hardly the only kinds of cases where the conventional approach comes up short. Outcomes in domestic-violence cases are often equally problematic. There is a good deal of evidence to suggest that courts have done little to deter continued violence in the home. Probation-violation rates in domestic-violence cases are disturbingly high, and the National Center for State Courts reports that 34 percent of batterers violate orders of protection.[13] The problem of recidivism is hardly confined to domestic violence. It is estimated that more than 50 percent of offenders convicted of drug possession will re-offend within three years.[14]

All of this bad news has led many jurists to conclude that the current system is broken. As New York State Chief Judge Judith S. Kaye has written:

> In many of today's cases, the traditional approach yields unsatisfying results. The addict arrested for drug dealing is adjudicated, does time, then goes right back to dealing on the street. The battered wife obtains a protective order, goes home, and is beaten again. Every legal right is protected, all procedures are followed, yet we aren't making a dent in the underlying problem. Not good for the parties involved. Not good for the community. Not good for the courts."[15]

Despite their best intentions, no matter which way they turn—to incarceration, probation, time-served sentences, or protective orders—judges are confronted with unappealing options.

THE RISING TIDE

The number of cases entering the American court system each year is staggering. According to the National Center for State Courts, from 1984 to 1998, criminal case filings increased by 50 percent. Adding more cases exacerbates all of the problems discussed above, further taxing an already overburdened criminal justice system. Evidence of this can be found in the newspaper coverage of courts from around the country. The headlines tell the story: "Anti-Crime Initiative Clogs Courts; Judges Fear Their Dockets Could Become Bottleneck" (*Washington Post*); "Court Change Fails to Unclog City's System" (*Baltimore Sun*); "County's Court Backlog Leads Innocent to Plead Guilty, Defenders Say," (*Durham Herald-Sun*).

But the bad news doesn't stop there. It's not just that there are more cases; it's that the kinds of cases that state courts are being asked to handle are increasingly difficult. The National Center for State Courts reports that the largest increases in case filings from 1984 to 1998 were in the areas of domestic relations (which grew by 75 percent) and in juvenile cases (up 73 percent). As a point of comparison, the United States population increased by 15 percent over those same years.[16] But these numbers are just the tip of the proverbial iceberg. The story is no different for quality-of-life crime. In New York City, for example, over the past decade the number of misdemeanor cases has increased by 85 percent.[17] And national research reveals that as many as three out of every four defendants in major American cities test positive for drugs at the time of arrest.[18]

All of this activity has led New York State Chief Judge Judith S. Kaye to write: "The numbers of cases in the state courts are huge. . . . There are not only more of them, but they've changed. . . . We're recycling the same people through the system. And things get worse. We know from experience that a drug possession or an assault today could be something considerably worse tomorrow."[19]

Where did all of these cases come from? For many, the rise in caseloads is a reflection of the rise of new social problems. For example, there's little doubt that the crack epidemic made a significant difference, bringing not only new drug cases into the system but related problems as well (e.g., child abuse and neglect cases involving addicted parents, or landlord-tenant disputes where a tenant fails to pay rent because of substance abuse).

Others credit the political branches for the jump in court activity. Certainly, the courts in places like New York City are feeling the effects of aggressive law-enforcement strategies as cops and prosecutors have cracked down on low-level miscreants (not to mention the impact of there simply being more police officers than ever before, thanks in no small part to the federal government's decision during the 1990s to add tens of thousands of new officers to local police departments). In other places, like Portland, Oregon, new and controversial laws have been passed to restrict the access of convicted offenders to certain public spaces (for example, a judge might issue a "stay away" order prohibiting a convicted prostitute from entering a neighborhood park). And across the country, mandatory arrest and "no-drop" prosecution policies have dramatically improved the likelihood that a domestic-violence incident will result in a court case.

By criminalizing behavior that up until recently would have received no criminal sanction—or simply by more aggressively enforcing laws already on the books—thousands of new cases have been brought into the system. But courts don't get to choose the cases that come in their doors—those decisions are made by the legislative branch, which writes the laws, and the executive branch, which enforces them.

"MCJUSTICE"

The court system is under tremendous pressure to absorb all these new cases and process them quickly—to make room for even more cases down the road. This means that for many judges, speed is the distinguishing feature of their work. And, in turn, the need for speed has taken a heavy toll on both the effectiveness of state courts and the morale of those who work in them.

New York judge Judy Harris Kluger tells this story: "For a long time, my claim to fame was that I arraigned 200 cases in one session. That's ridiculous. When I was arraigning cases, I'd be handed the papers, say the sentence is going to be five days, ten days, whatever, never even looking at the defendant."[20]

"Judges are very frustrated," says Kathleen Blatz, chief justice of the Minnesota Supreme Court,

> I think the innovation that we're seeing now is a result of judges processing cases like a vegetable factory. Instead of cans of peas, you've got cases. You just move 'em, move 'em, move 'em. One of my colleagues on the bench said, "You know, I feel like I work for McJustice: We sure aren't good for you, but we are fast."[21]

And judges aren't the only ones feeling the pinch. According to Lee H. Carson, a Cook County, Illinois, public defender,

> In the old days, you could sit down with a client. They'd tell you their life story until you got tired of hearing it, but you'd learn what they were about. But with the explosion of drug cases in particular, you have mass production. I'll have 110 barking guys in the lockup for preliminary hearings. If I gave each one of them five minutes, that would be nine hours before court. I couldn't do it. It's another case, another case, another case. It's like a sausage factory.[22]

Some have argued that the problem is a simple matter of resources, that we just need more judges and attorneys to meet the growth in caseload volume. An argument can be made that there's a serious mismatch between the demand for and the supply of court resources. To give just one example, in the 1990s, New York City's police force grew to include a record 40,000 officers. Meanwhile, the number of criminal court judges in the city has remained roughly the same since the mid-1970s.[23]

But the problems run deeper than that. Hire more judges and attorneys, renovate courthouses, upgrade court technology, but the reality will remain: in the bulk of cases that appear in state courts, the conventional approach does little to change the behavior of offenders, aid victims, or protect communities. Scott Newman, formerly the elected prosecutor of Indianapolis, talks about "the absurdity of managing only for process instead of for outcomes":

> Both prosecutors and police were tending to measure their performance by process—how fast we respond to 911 calls or how many cases we process—instead of measuring outcomes that really mattered to people, like whether they felt safer in their neighborhood or whether they were able to take a walk in the evening in their neighborhood. It struck me as kind of cynical on the part of police and prosecutors that they felt that there was nothing that they could do to affect the quality of life in the community.[24]

According to Patrick McGrath, a San Diego prosecutor, "I think it's fair to say there's a sense of yearning out there. If you grab a judge, a defense attorney and prosecutor and sat them down together and bought them a round of drinks, after a few beers, they'll all complain about the same thing: 'I have all this education and what do I do? I work in an assembly line. I don't affect case outcomes.' "[25]

What McGrath and Newman are describing, each in his own way, is revolving-door justice. Crucially, in both of their formulations the answer is not simply to reduce the number of cases within the system, even if that were in fact possible. Rather, Newman and McGrath are calling for judges and attorneys to reexamine what they do and how they do it, with an eye toward the ultimate impacts on victims, defendants, and communities.

While the number of judges and attorneys who are fed up with revolving-door justice is steadily growing, they still represent only a fraction of those who practice in American courts. All too many judges and attorneys express complete satisfaction with how the courts are currently working. A 1998 study of the courts in Los Angeles revealed that nine out of ten judges held a positive view of the court system. Unfortunately, there appears to be a disconnect between judges and the citizens they are supposed to serve: the same study revealed that among members of the public, only 17 percent of those surveyed had "strong confidence" in the system.[26]

THE CUSTOMER IS ALWAYS RIGHT

Sadly, the Los Angeles survey is not an anomaly: American courts routinely get low marks from the general public.

In 1999, the National Center for State Courts sponsored a national telephone survey that asked 1,826 Americans how they felt about state courts. While the results were by no means uniformly negative—respondents generally felt that courts do a good job of protecting defendants' constitutional rights and that judges are generally honest and fair—the levels of public trust and confidence in courts were disturbingly low. Only 23 percent expressed a great deal of trust in state courts. More people thought that the courts handled cases in a poor manner than thought that courts handled cases in an excellent manner.

Eighty percent of respondents agreed that "cases are not resolved in a timely manner." Over half agreed that "judges do not give adequate time and attention to each individual case" and that "courts do not make sure their orders are enforced." African Americans expressed particularly low levels of confidence in the system. Almost 70 percent thought that blacks, as a group, were treated worse in the court system than whites.[27] Going back a little further, a 1978 study revealed that courts dealing with minor criminal and juvenile matters receive more unfavorable ratings than civil and major criminal courts.[28]

In 1996, community-court planners in Red Hook, a low-income neighborhood in Brooklyn, New York, commissioned a door-to-door survey of local residents. The goal of the survey was to solicit information about perceptions of neighborhood quality-of-life, posing questions such as: What are the public-safety priorities in Red Hook? Are things getting better or worse here? How could a community court make a difference?

Along the way, respondents were asked what they thought of local criminal justice agencies. The percentage that rated courts positively was 12 percent. Even the police—not always a popular agency in low-income and minority neighborhoods—placed higher, with an underwhelming 14 percent approval rating. Even in an era of public cynicism about government, this amounts to a staggering vote of no confidence in the courts and in the criminal justice system.

It has become a mantra among those in the service industry that "the customer is always right." Unfortunately, courts don't usually think of citizens as customers to be served. Like any business that verges on being a monopoly, they've grown inured to customer complaints. But the courts ignore the feelings, desires, and needs of citizens at their own peril. As former Supreme Court justice Thurgood Marshall wrote, "We must never forget that the only real source of power that we as judges can tap is the respect of the people."[29]

Given Marshall's warning, courts should worry when citizens like Beverly Watts Davis, a community organizer in San Antonio, Texas, says: "Overall, people really do see the courts . . . as a problem creator."[30]

The bottom line is that our state-court system is plagued both by generations-old problems and by a new set of emerging challenges. Looking at today's state courts with their rote plea bargaining, overwhelming caseloads, and reliance on ineffective punishments, it is fair to ask: Have courts made our communities feel safer? Have they taken care of victims? Have they given defendants a sense that they will be treated with fairness? Sad to say, the answer appears to be no on all counts, which has led observers like Ellen Schall, the dean of New York University's Wagner School, to conclude, "I think we have to begin from the notion that the system from which the problem-solving courts have emerged was a failure on any count. It wasn't a legal success. It wasn't a social success. It wasn't working."[31]

2

What Are Problem-Solving Courts?

*Stability does not mean that we should be impervious
to change. Courts should be a stable institution,
but we should move forward to be relevant and meaningful
to the twenty-first-century problems in society. . . .
Sometimes things aren't broken, they just don't work
optimally. And if we can make them work better,
then why shouldn't we go ahead and make changes?*

—JUDITH S. KAYE, Chief Judge, New York State[1]

The last decade has been a time of unprecedented court
innovation. Hundreds of new judicial experiments have
opened their doors. These have included community courts
that seek to improve the quality of life in neighborhoods
struggling with crime and disorder; drug courts that attempt
to stop the cycle of drugs, crime, and jail for addicted offenders; and domestic-violence courts that shine a spotlight on a
group of cases—violence between intimates—that have historically received short shrift from the justice system.

All told, more than two thousand problem-solving courts are currently in operation, with dozens more in the planning stages. Some handle serious felonies; others handle minor misdemeanor cases. Some look very much like conventional courtrooms; others handle their business in neighborhood-based facilities that resemble community centers as much as courthouses.

Some problem-solving courts use the authority of the court to link offenders to therapeutic interventions (e.g., drug courts), while in others, the goal is to strengthen traditional punishments, making sure that sanctions have real teeth (e.g., domestic-violence courts).

In some of the new courts, defenders and prosecutors work as a team to help offenders in treatment. In others, the adversarial process is basically unchanged. Some are essentially part-time courtrooms, handling limited dockets a few afternoons each week, while others are among the busiest courtrooms in the country, handling thousands of cases each year.

The diversity doesn't end there. Some of the new judicial experiments have been underwritten by local and state government. Others rely on federal funding. Judicial experimentation has occurred in conservative and rural jurisdictions that tend to vote Republican, and it has occurred in liberal and industrial states that typically vote Democrat.

Given this diversity—of method, location, caseload, architecture, funding, and process—it's worth asking: What do all of these initiatives have in common?

Each shares an underlying premise: that courts should do more than just process cases, that at the end of the day, the goal is not just to make it through the calendar, but to make a difference in the lives of victims, the lives of defendants, and the lives of neighborhoods. In one way or another, all of the new judicial experiments are attempting to solve the kinds of cases where social, human, and legal problems intersect.

The potential implications of this shift in orientation are profound. Problem-solving courts recognize that to dispose of a case is not the same thing as to resolve it. As a consequence, they do not restrict themselves to the standard approach to case processing—a framework that often obscures the problems that brought a defendant to court, the long-term impacts of offending on a neighborhood, and the harms suffered by victims.

Problem-solving courts ask judges and attorneys to do more than just apply the law correctly. Problem-solving courts demand that everyone attached to the court broaden their scope to see the real-life consequences of courtroom decisions. And they insist that courts use data to make more informed decisions about where to target resources and how to craft effective sanctions. Those who practice problem-solving justice are committed to seeing each individual case in the context of the lives of victims, communities, and defendants.

THE SHOPLIFTING EXAMPLE

Not all shoplifters are created equal. Some are teenagers testing limits with their friends. Others are thieves who boost for a living. Still others are long-term drug users who steal to support their addictions. Should each of these offenders receive the same sanction? Shouldn't judges and attorneys have the tools to respond differently in each of these cases? While proportionality—making sure a punishment fits the crime—is important, there's no reason why justice has to be one-size-fits-all.

A commitment to problem solving means taking a deeper look at the victim as well. In the case of shoplifting, the

relevant questions might be: Has this store-owner been victimized before? How often? Should police officers be paying
special attention to this location? A problem-solving lawyer
or judge might broaden his scope even further and begin to
ask whether shoplifting is a chronic problem in the neighborhood and what kinds of prevention measures might be
brought to bear. In short, problem-solving judges and attorneys insist on seeing life in 3-D.

While the fullest articulation of the problem-solving concept to date can be found in lower-level criminal cases like
shoplifting, this application represents just the tip of the iceberg. Is it possible to imagine a problem-solving approach to
more serious crimes? To federal cases?[2] To civil cases? Is it
possible to train young lawyers to be problem solvers instead
of kill-or-be-killed litigators? Advocates of problem-solving
justice are currently attempting all of the above.

PRINCIPLES

As currently practiced in specialized courtrooms across the
country, the hallmarks of problem-solving justice include:

• *Redefining Goals*. Problem-solving courts define success in
  new ways. No longer is it enough for judges and attorneys
  to focus exclusively on process and precedents. Instead,
  problem-solving justice demands that courts think deeply
  about the outcomes they achieve for victims, for offenders,
  and for society. Depending upon the court, these might
  include reductions in recidivism, reduced stays in foster
  care for children, increased sobriety for addicts, and safer
  and cleaner neighborhoods. This idea, that judges and
  attorneys should take into consideration the context from
  which cases arise and think about the long-term impacts of

courtroom decisions, may not, at first blush, seem like a radical notion. But, in the context of courts, which exalt fairness and impartiality as the highest possible virtues, it is indeed a significant departure from business as usual. In practice, what this really means is that judges and prosecutors and defenders are redefining their goals. The judge in a problem-solving court is not just worried about managing the process. The prosecutor is not just concerned with locking up "bad guys." And the defense attorney is not just looking to get her client off. Instead, they are all saying that the goal of court is to improve public safety by addressing neighborhood hot spots, aiding victims, and changing the behavior of offenders while also protecting their rights. In the words of former Indianapolis prosecutor Scott Newman, problem-solving courts ensure that courts keep an eye on both outcomes and process simultaneously.

- *Making the Most of Judicial Authority*. Problem-solving courts make aggressive use of a largely untapped resource: the power of judges to promote compliance with court orders. Instead of passing off cases after rendering a sentence— to other judges, to probation departments, to community-based treatment programs or, in all too many cases, to no one at all—judges in problem-solving courts stay involved with each case over the long haul. Drug-court judges, for example, closely supervise the performance of offenders in drug treatment, requiring them to return to court frequently for urine testing and courtroom progress reports. There is a great deal of evidence that offenders take what judges say very seriously. Put simply, they are more likely to show up, to keep clean and sober, and to stay out of trouble when a judge is checking up on them (as opposed to a probation or parole officer or a counselor). This idea, using judicial authority to strengthen accountability, has been central to the success of problem-solving courts.

- *Putting Problems in Context.* Building on the model of problem-oriented policing, problem-solving courts seek to move beyond handling cases as isolated incidents. Rather, they recognize that court cases are often symptoms of larger social and neighborhood problems. Problem-solving courts seek to gain a deeper understanding of the issues that are fueling court caseloads, on the theory that more information leads to better judicial decision-making. This can be seen in the insistence that judges in domestic-violence courts receive special training in the unique dynamics of domestic violence. Or the way that community courts inform judges about neighborhood hot spots and eyesores. Or the way that drug-court judges are asked to understand basic pharmacology. The emphasis on information can also be seen in the efforts of many problem-solving courts to use computer technology to make sure that judges have access to in-depth profiles of defendants, and the use of research data to measure court impacts.

- *Forming Creative Partnerships.* Problem-solving courts employ a collaborative, multidisciplinary approach, relying on both government and nonprofit partners (social scientists, treatment providers, probation departments, community groups, and others) to help achieve their goals. For example, domestic-violence courts have developed partnerships with batterers' programs and probation departments to help improve the monitoring of defendants. Community courts have engaged in aggressive crime-prevention efforts, working with local public-housing authorities and tenant associations to fix broken locks and windows in public-housing developments. And many problem-solving courts rely on technologists and researchers to help judges make better decisions and distinguish which sanctions are most effective. The idea here is that problem-solving courts seek to open the courthouse doors, bringing new tools and new ways of thinking into the courtroom.

- *Rethinking Traditional Roles.* Problem-solving courts don't just introduce new players into the courthouse; they also ask existing players to take on new roles. For example, at many drug courts, attorneys on both sides of the aisle are asked to work together to determine who is eligible to participate and to craft systems of sanctions and rewards for offenders in drug treatment. This unprecedented collaboration between the prosecution and the defense bar doesn't end in the planning stages, it continues through implementation, as attorneys work together to encourage offenders to succeed in treatment. All of these changes in role definition—some subtle, some profound—emerge as a consequence of problem-solving courts' rearticulation of the bottom line, of what the goal of court is. For drug-court attorneys, the measure of success has become not whether they win or lose the case, but whether they are able to change the dysfunctional behavior of addicted offenders and reduce recidivism. Attorneys are not the only ones whose roles have changed. Many problem-solving courts have asked judges to play the roles of convener and broker, using their authority to coordinate the work of other agencies. For example, some drug-court judges have been quite aggressive in working with drug-treatment providers (and regulatory agencies), encouraging them to change their practices to meet the special needs of drug-court participants (e.g., by creating more in-patient slots or offering special treatment options for addicts who are also mentally ill).

Whether one feels that problem solving is consistent with traditional judicial practice or a radical departure from it, one of the movement's distinguishing features is that it cannot be easily reduced to a single way of thinking. In some cases, a problem-solving approach demands a focus on rehabilitation, on helping an offender cure what ails him or her. In other cases, a problem-solving perspective foregrounds the need to protect victims and tighten the accountability of offenders. In others, the problem-solving approach privileges the community, a class of people who aren't even party to the case at hand. But in all cases, problem-solving justice demands that courts define a goal (e.g., to reduce substance abuse among addicted offenders or to reduce crime in a particular neighborhood) and then adjust procedures to achieve that bottom line.

Seen in one light, problem solving lacks firm definition and runs the risk of becoming all things to all people—any deviation from the norm can be branded "problem-solving." A more constructive view sees problem solving as offering judges and lawyers a creative, multidisciplinary approach to resolving disputes and solving problems.

ORIGINS

Generally speaking, problem-solving courts have emerged without centralized planning or leadership, in more or less spontaneous fashion, as hundreds of judges and attorneys throughout the country have attempted, by trial and error, to fashion new responses to a set of common problems. There was no presidential call to arms, organized political campaign, or landmark scholarship that called these new experiments into being. Nor is there a governing body or regulatory agency for problem-solving courts (although it is fair to say that the U.S. Department of Justice under both President Clinton and President Bush has played a major role in seeding the field through grant-making, publicity, technical assistance, and research).[3]

The problem-solving movement represents a pastiche of good ideas and interesting strategies borrowed from other disciplines and other movements, including alternative dispute resolution, the victims' movement, reforms like problem-oriented and broken-windows policing, therapeutic jurisprudence, and juvenile court. In both theory and in practice, these developments have set the stage for problem-solving courts.[4] What follows is a look at each of these precursors.

ALTERNATIVE DISPUTE RESOLUTION

Alternative dispute resolution is an unwieldy, catch-all phrase that describes a variety of nonviolent mechanisms for resolving conflict (e.g., arbitration, facilitation, conciliation) that do not rely on the edifice of the law or the adversarial process. The most basic of these is mediation, a process that brings two parties in conflict together to discuss their differences. A neutral third-party serves as a referee, helping to guide the parties to a mutually beneficial agreement about how to resolve the problem at hand (and helping them avoid the costs and the delays that typically come with litigation).

Mediation is often used to handle minor criminal and civil cases involving neighbors, relatives, and acquaintances—charges of harassment, minor assaults, business disputes, and the like. Given the ongoing relationship between the parties in these cases, traditional sanctions—fines and incarceration—tend not to satisfy anyone. The appeal of mediation is based on a critique of the traditional adversarial system.

Advocates of mediation often claim that it is a win-win process, in which both sides can claim at least partial victory. This stands in stark contrast to the either/or nature of the adversarial process, with its need to determine clear winners and losers. Whether the dispute in question involves neighbors arguing over noise, schoolmates in a fight about a girlfriend, or a formerly married couple in a conflict over visitation rights, the goal of mediation is to empower the parties to take responsibility for their own actions rather than having solutions imposed upon them by authority figures, and to seek to find mutually beneficial outcomes instead of playing a zero-sum game.

One of the most ambitious efforts to test the practical applications of mediation occurred in the late 1970s with the creation of a number of community mediation programs around the country. Spurred in large measure by federal funding from the U.S. Department of Justice, community mediation programs sought to improve neighborhoods by addressing local conflicts among residents. The early proponents of community mediation argued that these programs would help reduce court caseloads, encourage self-governance, and improve public confidence in justice.

After more than a generation of practice, community mediation has proven remarkably durable and adaptable. From a handful of experiments, the field has grown to include more than four hundred programs, offering a diverse array of services. Those who participate in mediation tend to like it. Most programs have no problem attracting volunteers to serve as mediators. And community mediation earns high marks from disputants for fairness and speed, especially when compared to court-case processing.

But many within the field have expressed concerns about quality control. Community mediation programs tend to rely on volunteer mediators, which raises all sorts of issues about qualifications and training. More fundamentally, community mediation programs have not been able to demonstrate the kind of results that generate enthusiasm over the long haul from policy makers, funders, or academics. Even when a case is successfully mediated and two combatants sign a written agreement, it's unclear how long the mediation fix lasts. One study that looked at divorce mediation found that any positive short-term impacts from mediation tended to dissipate over time. Two years following the divorce, those who participated in mediation did not report different levels of cooperation, conflict, or compliance rates than those who pursued more conventional court remedies.[5]

Although many community mediation programs were created as diversion programs, to siphon cases out of the traditional system, there is little evidence that they have managed to reduce the volume of cases coming into courts (or court costs, for that matter).[6] And many mediation programs suffer from frighteningly high attrition rates. Because mediation is a voluntary process, many disputants simply opt out, choosing to seek their day in court instead. Community mediation is, at the end of the day, a movement framed by a fundamental paradox: the societal need for mediation may be large (conflicts are, after all, not exactly in short supply these days), but the public demand is relatively low.[7]

Though less than an unequivocal success, community mediation has opened the door for problem-solving courts in a couple of important respects. First, mediation has underlined the importance of low-level criminal and civil disputes, cases that often receive little attention from judges and attorneys. It has also highlighted some of the deficiencies of the adversarial process, encouraging new thinking about how to approach certain kinds of legal problems. Advocates of alter-native dispute resolution have also made significant inroads into the legal curriculum; mediation is now taught at hun-dreds of law schools. Problem-solving courts have benefited immeasurably from this—it has helped give problem-solving courts credibility and created a cadre of lawyers who are trained to think about problems in new ways.

Community courts in particular owe a sizable debt to community mediation programs. The two share a basic belief that justice should be decentralized, moved out of downtown office complexes and into the neighborhoods directly affected by crime and disorder. They also share a desire to reinvigorate citizen involvement, engaging local residents as mediators, community advisory board mem-bers, and volunteers.

For all of problem-solving courts' connections to media-tion, it is important to note at least one crucial difference. Most mediation programs are conceived of as alternatives to court.[8] They are, almost by definition, voluntary programs. The weakness of this approach is twofold: many mediation programs do not have a solid institutional base, and, as we have seen, many struggle with caseload volume issues.

By contrast, problem-solving courts are part of the for-mal criminal justice system. They seek not to divert cases out of the system but rather to reengineer the system itself. In the process, they make use of the coercive authority of courts, mandating offenders into treatment, community-restitution projects, and other sanctions (even, on occa-sion, mediation!). The early indications are that these fac-tors may help inoculate problem-solving courts against some of the problems that have befallen community medi-ation programs.

THE VICTIMS' MOVEMENT

One unexpected consequence of the rise in crime throughout the 1960s and 1970s was the emergence of victims as a recognizable constituency, with a political voice all its own.[9] Starting in the 1960s (and continuing to this day), victims of crime have consistently assailed a criminal justice system that places defendants at center stage while all but ignoring victims. Many speak of being victimized twice: once by the perpetrator and then again by police, prosecutors, and judges who violate their privacy, deny claims for reparation, and fail to notify them or allow them a voice when crucial decisions are made.

In response to these concerns, the victims' movement has waged a battle simultaneously on a number of fronts: building public awareness, lobbying for legislative change, and providing direct services to those in need of assistance. As this breadth of activity implies, the victims' movement is a loose amalgam of hundreds of rape-crisis centers, victim-service agencies, battered-women's shelters, victim-compensation programs, and victims'-rights campaigns with names like Protect the Innocent, Parents of Murdered Children, and Mothers Against Drunk Driving.

The collective achievements of these organizations are astounding. From the creation of the first victim-assistance organization in St. Louis in 1972, it was just nine short years until President Ronald Reagan, in 1981, declared the existence of "Crime Victims' Week." Three years later, the Victims of Crime Act of 1984 created a formal federal agency, the Justice Department's Office for Victims of Crime, to provide ongoing funding for victim programs. Today, all fifty states have passed victims' bills of rights, and the Justice Department has established a special office, the Office on Violence Against Women, for dealing with domestic violence.

One of the most interesting, albeit controversial, out-growths of the victims' movement has been the emergence of "restorative justice." According to Mark Umbreit, a professor of social work at the University of Minnesota,

> Restorative justice is a victim-centered response to crime that provides opportunities for those most directly affected by crime—the victim, the offender, their families, and representatives of the community—to be directly involved in responding to the harm caused by the crime. Restorative justice [emphasizes] the importance of . . . offering support and assistance to crime victims; holding offenders directly accountable to the people and communities they have violated; restoring the emotional and material losses of victims (to the degree possible); providing a range of opportunities for dialogue and problem solving . . . offering offenders opportunities for competency development and reintegration into productive community life; and strengthening public safety through community building.[10]

Examples of restorative justice include victim-offender mediation, family group conferencing, reparative probation, sentencing circles, community-restitution programs, and many other efforts to restore the health of victims and neighborhoods while offering offenders a chance to "earn back their place in society."[11] Not everyone within the victims' movement is a fan of restorative justice—there are many who are not especially keen to "restore" offenders. In the eyes of its proponents, however, restorative justice is an antidote to the "retributive" model of justice that is currently ascendant in the United States.

Little research exists to measure the success of restorative-justice programs.[12] There are, however, some signs that suggest that victims who participate in restorative justice are significantly more satisfied with the process and the outcome. There is also evidence that points to reduced levels of fear among victims and an increased sense of fairness among offenders.[13]

What elements have problem-solving courts taken from restorative justice and the victims' movement in general? Certainly, problem-solving courts' focus on improving the safety of victims (domestic-violence courts) and restoring the harm done to communities (community courts) grows directly out of the victims' movement. In fact, one of the underlying principles that drives the nation's three dozen community courts is the idea that neighborhoods can be victimized by crime just as individuals can, and that crimes like prostitution and drug sales, previously thought of as "victimless," do indeed have a victim: the community.

Problem-solving courts have also benefited from the political groundwork that victim advocates have put in place. In fact, many problem-solving initiatives, particularly those that target domestic violence, have relied on funding from the federal bureaucracies that the victims' movement helped to create—the Office for Victims of Crime, and the Office on Violence Against Women at the U.S. Department of Justice. Problem-solving courts have also embraced the victims' movement's emphasis on including different stakeholders in the criminal justice process beyond the traditional work group of judges, cops, and attorneys. The victims' movement helped open the doors not only for victims, but for victim advocates, social-service providers, and community groups to have a voice in the system.

Finally, problem-solving courts have built upon the political flexibility of the victims' movement. The success of the victims' movement was aided and abetted at key moments by making common cause with feminist organizations (which, among other things, focused attention on the crimes of rape and domestic violence) and with law-and-order conservatives (who pressed for stiffer punishments for offenders). Similarly, problem-solving courts have made allies across the political spectrum, from liberals who believe in rehabilitation to conservatives who espouse order maintenance. It remains to be seen whether this recipe will guarantee problem-solving courts the same kind of resilience and long-term success that the victims' movement has enjoyed.

PROBLEM-ORIENTED POLICING AND THE BROKEN WINDOWS THEORY

Problem-oriented policing is a conceptual framework first articulated by Herman Goldstein, a researcher at the University of Wisconsin Law School. Goldstein's experience examining beleaguered police departments in the 1970s impressed upon him that to improve performance, "the police were going to have to cultivate an entirely different type of relationship with the citizens they served."[14]

The answer, according to Goldstein, is "problem-oriented policing," a prescription that calls for police to understand their work in a new light. Instead of merely responding to incidents—a robbery, a fight, a noise complaint, teenagers loitering on the corner—on a case-by-case basis, Goldstein argues that police need to look for patterns among incidents and understand the context in which they occur:

> The first step in problem-oriented policing is to move beyond just handling incidents. It calls for recognizing that incidents are often merely overt symptoms of problems. This pushes the police in two directions: (1) It requires that

they recognize the relationships between incidents (similarities of behavior, location, persons involved, etc.); and (2) it requires that they take a more in-depth interest in incidents by acquainting themselves with some of the conditions and factors that give rise to them.[15]

At the heart of problem-oriented policing are four basic components: 1) identifying problems (Goldstein encourages the police to look first to the community to nominate problems); 2) analyzing problems (collecting information and conducting a rigorous inquiry into the nature of the problem, be it a wave of car thefts, home break-ins, or gang violence); 3) searching for alternative solutions (looking for effective ways to deal with the problem, including nonenforcement strategies); and 4) measuring effectiveness (assessing the success or failure of the solution).

The bottom line for Goldstein is a desire to improve police effectiveness, to encourage police to measure success in ways other than simply counting the number of arrests they make. But in calling for increased scrutiny of police outcomes, Goldstein is extremely sober about how police officers work and what they can realistically be expected to achieve. It is no accident that he labels his concept problem-*oriented* policing rather than problem-*solving*. "It makes no sense," he writes,

> . . . to equate effectiveness to solving problems, for the problems are seldom eliminated. . . . For much of police business, . . . a more realistic goal is to reduce the number of incidents that a problem creates and to reduce the seriousness of these incidents. That is why it is helpful to characterize the police role more realistically as *managing deviance* and then concentrate on equipping the police to carry out this management role with greater effectiveness.[16]

Goldstein was hardly the only innovative thinker to put his mind to police operations in the 1980s. Indeed, the past generation has been a golden era for police reformers. Problem-oriented policing has been forced to compete in the marketplace of ideas with a range of other police reform efforts, initiatives with names like "zero tolerance," "community policing," "pulling levers," "hot-spot policing," and "broken-windows policing."[17]

It would take a Talmudic scholar to parse the differences among these overlapping theories (not to mention the competing claims of their originators and implementers). While all have their devotees, perhaps the single most influential criminal justice idea of the past generation is the "broken windows" theory.

Published in 1982, "Broken Windows: The Police and Neighborhood Safety," an article in *The Atlantic Monthly* by James Q. Wilson and George L. Kelling of Harvard University, suggests that police officers should focus renewed attention on conditions of neighborhood disorder like graffiti, broken windows, and drunk and disorderly individuals. The theory is that when these problems are left unaddressed, it sends a message to potential criminals that more serious wrongdoing is permissible. In this way, low-level disorder and serious crime are inextricably linked.[18]

In recent years, police departments have taken this idea to heart, cracking down on low-level offenses on the street and in the subways. Many credit this renewed vigilance with precipitating the remarkable drops in crime that cities like New York have experienced over the past decade.

While broken-windows policing is now part of the standard vocabulary of criminal justice officials in this country, the progress of problem-oriented policing has been, in the words of a Justice Department report, "slow, modest and uneven."[19] Advocates of problem-oriented policing have struggled to figure out how to implement Goldstein's ideas, particularly with regard to training officers, accessing improved data, and crafting effective partnerships with other government agencies.[20]

While broken-windows and problem-oriented policing have followed different paths, problem-solving courts have borrowed language and concepts from both. Most significantly, building on these policing innovations, problem-solving courts are insistent that courts need to stop counting cases and instead measure their effectiveness by the outcomes they achieve. Problem-solving courts' emphasis on low-level crime, their focus on sparking the creativity of system insiders, their reliance on rigorous research and analysis, and their desire to build new partnerships are all straight out of the broken-windows and problem-oriented policing playbook. And so is their call to judges and lawyers to think beyond the immediate case in front of them to see the big picture. In all of these ways, problem-solving courts stand on the shoulders of broken-windows and problem-oriented policing.

THERAPEUTIC JURISPRUDENCE

In the words of its two most visible champions, law professors Bruce Winick and David Wexler,

> Therapeutic jurisprudence is the study of the role of the law as a therapeutic agent. . . . Legal rules, legal procedures and the roles of legal actors (such as lawyers and judges) constitute social forces that, like it or not, often produce therapeutic or anti-therapeutic consequences. Therapeutic jurisprudence proposes that we be sensitive to those consequences, and that we ask whether the law's anti-therapeutic

consequences can be reduced, and its therapeutic consequences enhanced, without subordinating due process and
other justice values."[21]

More narrowly, therapeutic jurisprudence has been defined
as "the use of social science to study the extent to which a
legal rule or practice promotes the psychological and physical well-being of the people it affects."[22]

Therapeutic jurisprudence emerged out of mental-
health law in the late 1980s. Since then, it has gained a
wider audience, steadily picking up academic proponents
along the way. In the process, therapeutic jurisprudence
has been applied to an ever-widening array of legal concerns, including health care, family law, tort reform, sentencing guidelines, and jury instructions.

Therapeutic jurisprudence offers a unique lens through
which to view the interactions in a typical criminal courtroom. For example, a judge with an interest in promoting
therapeutic outcomes might choose to allow victims to speak
in open court as a way of promoting emotional closure and
healing. Or, more provocatively, based on behavioral science
research that indicates that individuals who commit acts of
domestic violence frequently deny responsibility for their
behavior, a therapeutic judge might require offenders to provide details about their offenses in open court as a way of
insuring that they accept responsibility for their crime.[23]

In addition to looking at individual cases, therapeutic
jurisprudence can be applied to issues of court policy and
organization. For example, by labeling people "offenders,"
do competency hearings have a deleterious impact on their
behavior? How should family courts be organized to reduce
the stress that multiple court appearances place on families in crisis?

While therapeutic jurisprudence has produced volumes of scholarly interest (the bible of the field, *Law in a Therapeutic Key*, clocks in at a hefty 1,012 pages and features dozens of contributors), it hasn't as yet generated a lot of action. There are relatively few real-life examples of practitioners deliberately applying therapeutic jurisprudence principles to their work.

Perhaps because of this, in recent years some problem-solving judges and attorneys have seized upon therapeutic jurisprudence as a way to justify their actions. For example, in an article titled "Therapeutic Jurisprudence and the Drug Treatment Court Movement: Revolutionizing the Criminal Justice System's Response to Drug Abuse and Crime in America," judges Peggy Hora and William Schma (along with co-author John Rosenthal) argue that "without being conscious of its use" drug courts have been applying therapeutic jurisprudence to the problems of addicted criminal defendants. Thus, therapeutic jurisprudence provides "the legal and jurisprudential foundations of this new criminal justice concept."[24] Some domestic-violence court and mental-health court practitioners have also come to view their work through the prism of therapeutic jurisprudence.

These problem-solvers have been attracted to therapeutic jurisprudence for good reasons: it's outcome-oriented, multidisciplinary, emphasizes empirically verifiable results, and asks practitioners to think outside of the confines of individual cases. That's all part and parcel of the daily work of problem-solving courts.

But at the end of the day, therapeutic jurisprudence and problem-solving courts are something less than a perfect fit. Some advocates of therapeutic jurisprudence worry that problem-solving courts are imperfect vehicles for advancing their aims and that problem-solving courts may distract attention from other potential applications of the therapeutic lens.

On the other side of the ledger, some problem-solving practitioners blanch at the term therapeutic jurisprudence. Their
concerns are twofold. First, they worry that therapeutic
jurisprudence is a political liability as a label, an instant
turnoff for those who will immediately conjure images of
judges leading twelve-step programs.

More substantively, there is a concern that the therapeutic label does not adequately describe either the origins
or the methods of problem-solving courts, that it places
these courts too squarely in the business of rehabilitation.
Many problem-solving courts rely on therapeutic interventions to change the behavior of offenders, of course, but
many others do not. Much of what problem-solving courts
do—improving judicial access to information, say, or tight-
ening the accountability measures for offenders released
on bail—has no explicit therapeutic dimension. The point
here is not to argue that there is no overlap between problem-
solving courts and therapeutic justice, but rather to suggest
that the relationship is more complicated than it appears
at first glance.

JUVENILE COURT

In 1899, the Illinois legislature passed the Juvenile Court Act,
providing for the creation of the first juvenile court in the
country. From there the idea spread quickly. Today, every
state has a separate court with jurisdiction over juveniles
who violate criminal laws. The rapid growth of juvenile
courts was fueled, at least in part, by the active championing
of the Progressive Movement, a band of child-centered
reformers who were also responsible for creating settlement
houses, launching kindergartens, and lobbying for the pas-
sage of child-labor laws.

The animating idea of the juvenile court was that young people needed to be treated differently than adults and that the justice system should attempt to act in the "best interests" of children. Julian Mack, one of the original juvenile court judges in Chicago, explained that the goal of juvenile court was to concern itself not with the specific charge facing the delinquent, but rather with "what he is, physically, mentally, morally, and then, if he is treading the path that leads to criminality," to move aggressively, "not so much to punish as to reform, not to degrade but to uplift, not to crush but to develop, to make him not a criminal but a worthy citizen."[25] Or, as the U.S. Department Justice's Office of Juvenile Justice and Delinquency Prevention put it nearly a century later, "The juvenile court system is based on the principle that youth are developmentally different from adults and more amenable to intervention."[26]

In an effort to make a difference in the lives of wayward youth, juvenile court judges were initially given broad discretion. The rules of adversarialism that governed adult criminal cases—the right to counsel, the right to cross-examine witnesses, the right to a speedy trial—were either relaxed or dispensed with entirely. Judges were encouraged to give each young person individualized attention and, in the process, to address the environmental factors (e.g., poverty, intemperance, lack of education in the home) that seemed to be linked to delinquent behavior.

The arguments employed by advocates of juvenile courts in their founding years will be familiar to any problem-solving judge or attorney. Juvenile court reformers believed in creating intermediate sanctions between jail and unfettered release, arguing that judges should look for the "least restrictive" outcome in each case. They argued that courts were uniquely qualified to oversee the work of social-service providers. They encouraged judges to make use of outside experts, particularly child psychologists, when crafting sentences. They believed that judges would make more informed decisions if they had access to additional information about a juvenile offender's background, home life, and neighborhood. They even advocated for a revisioning of courthouse architecture to make it more user-friendly and to include room for all of the various agencies engaged with helping kids. All of these ideas appear, in one form or another, in the literature of problem-solving reformers.

The rhetoric of juvenile court advocates was remarkably persuasive. In the early days, the juvenile court was embraced with near unanimity by politicians, citizens, and criminal-justice practitioners across ideological lines. Recent years have not been kind to juvenile courts, however; they have been under siege from both the left and the right for more than a generation.

Law-and-order conservatives have argued that juvenile courts are too lenient, that they offer juvenile offenders little more than a slap on the wrist. This argument has led many to advocate for removing serious offenders from the juvenile justice system. Today, all fifty states have provisions that allow juveniles to be tried as adults under certain circumstances. In addition, many states have passed laws introducing mandatory sentences for certain kinds of offenses and reducing the confidentiality provisions that have traditionally protected juvenile proceedings. The net effect has been to move juvenile courts a considerable distance from their original mission of benevolent rehabilitation.[27]

Juvenile courts were even more fundamentally altered by civil libertarians who argued that these courts were guilty of taking the concept of *parens patriae* (the state as parent) beyond acceptable limits. These critics derided the juvenile court for its paternalism and its lack of procedural protections. Perhaps the most telling blow was delivered by the U.S. Supreme Court in a 1967 case involving a fifteen-year-old boy who had been arrested for making a crank call and was committed by a juvenile court judge to a training school until he reached adulthood. Tellingly, the alleged victim did not appear at the hearing, and the court never resolved whether the boy had in fact made the offending phone call.

Acknowledging these lapses, the U.S. Supreme Court's decision, *In re Gault,* established that juveniles have a right to notice and counsel, to question witnesses, and to protection against self-incrimination. Subsequent Supreme Court decisions have added additional due-process safeguards, with the result that today's juvenile courts are often hard to distinguish from their adult criminal-court counterparts.

For all the problems that juvenile courts have faced lately, it is worth noting that their underlying assumption—that children who engage in delinquent behavior require special attention that is different from the criminal justice process for adults—continues to hold sway today. Given the obvious parallels, some encouraging, some unsettling, between juvenile courts and today's problem-solving courts, it is worth noting at least four important differences:

1   *Role of Defenders:* Problem-solving courts, at least the ones that are any good, have taken special pains to involve defense attorneys at the earliest possible stage of their development. As a result, problem-solving courts have been sensitive to issues of due process and proportionality, working hard to ensure that punishments fit the crime. (Some problem-solving courts, such as drug courts, also seek to ensure that punishments are less retributive than the ones offenders would receive in conventional courtrooms.) This

has helped win over some of the skeptics within the defense bar. Perhaps the best example of this comes from New York. Speaking at the opening of a domestic-violence court in the Bronx, Daniel Greenberg, then president of the New York City Legal Aid Society, said, "We were skeptical, but these courts have shown themselves capable of understanding that defendants have rights. . . . We too believe we're a problem-solving organization."

2   *Increased Accountability:* Over the past century, the success or failure of most juvenile courts has been heavily dependent upon probation. As Judge Richard Tuthill, Chicago's first juvenile court judge observed, probation is "the cord upon which all the pearls of the juvenile court are strung. . . . Without it, the juvenile court would not exist."[28] Unfortunately, probation departments have, by and large, turned out to be faulty vehicles—underresourced and overwhelmed with staggering caseloads, many probation departments have found it difficult to identify innovative interventions, to develop meaningful connections with community-based treatment providers, or to make informed decisions about which offenders require the most intensive supervision. The result has been that treatment sanctions have tended to lack teeth. Offenders have suffered few consequences unless they get arrested again. Recognizing this, problem-solving courts have attempted to bolster the monitoring of offenders by introducing judges into the mix. The resulting burden on judicial resources is not insignificant, but by requiring offenders to return to court regularly to report on their progress, problem-solving courts have markedly improved compliance. In an effort to assess the benefits of this approach, researchers are increasingly devoting their attention to studying the cost-effectiveness of the problem-solving model (see chapter 6).

3 *Measuring Impacts:* The notion that government initiatives should have clearly stated goals and should measure their success in attaining them seems obvious, but in truth it is a relatively new phenomenon. Juvenile court reformers did not face the kind of scrutiny that government reformers today must navigate—including questions about costs and benefits and long-term results. Nor did the reformers of yesteryear have access to the kinds of tools—most notably, computer technology—that would enable broad-scale data collection and analysis. Today's problem-solving innovators do. As a consequence, most problem-solving courts have not only articulated a set of measurable goals for themselves, they have also put in place the technological infrastructure needed to capture this data on an ongoing basis. Problem-solving courts are stronger as a result. With the help of technology, they are able to demonstrate their effectiveness in a way that juvenile courts could not.

4 *Realistic Aspirations:* The initial advocates of the juvenile court were not exactly shy about using the coercive authority of the state. A 1901 speech by Martha Falconer, a Chicago probation officer, is emblematic: "The women who cannot control their boys . . . should not have the care of them. . . .To those women I say, 'You will keep your children off the streets or the city of Chicago will do it for you.' "[29] In their desire to aid poor and immigrant children, progressive reformers were both exceedingly comfortable with the moral righteousness of their cause and supremely confident in the state's ability to intervene productively. With the benefit of hindsight, it is easy to see how these two things got the juvenile court into trouble. The fervor of today's court innovators has been tempered by a century's worth of experience with failed social interventions. Problem-solving

judges and attorneys, while eager to make good use of treatment providers, are much more realistic about the capacity
of contemporary experts and institutions to change behavior.
Or, to put it another way, problem solvers have not placed all
their eggs in the rehabilitation basket. They do not contend
that sentencing a shoplifter to paint over graffiti in the local
subway station is going to alter a lifetime of drug use and
homelessness. But they do argue that making low-level
offenders perform visible restitution is a better outcome for
the community than nothing at all or a few days in jail.

In all of these ways, problem-solving courts are well posi-
tioned to avoid some of the problems that have befallen
juvenile courts over the years.

3

Problem-Solving Courts in Action: Community Courts in New York and Oregon

When I was first elected District Attorney, I thought
I knew best. I went out to the neighborhoods and I just
knew that murders, rapes, and armed robberies
were the most important thing to residents. They handed
me my lunch. They talked about quality-of-life crimes.
I think that's what led me to push strongly for . . .
community courts—a desire to get out there and re-establish
the rule of law in the community.

—MICHAEL SCHRUNK, District Attorney,
Multnomah County, Oregon[1]

Of the three primary types of problem-solving courts—drug courts, domestic-violence courts, and community courts—community courts are perhaps the most ambitious. Not only do they attempt to change the way that judges, attorneys, and defendants interact in the courtroom, but they also seek to reach out to citizens, engaging them in the process of doing justice. In this chapter, we offer case studies of three separate community courts—two in New York and one in Oregon—whose stories paint a vivid picture of problem-solving justice in action.

TIMES SQUARE

It's difficult to remember now, but back in 1990, midtown Manhattan was, in the words of one local newspaper, "a den of prostitutes, crack dealing and crime." Pre-Disney, pre-Giuliani, pre–Internet boom, the central business district in New York City was not exactly the most hospitable place in town. In fact, the word most often used to describe the neighborhood was "seedy." Porn palaces outnumbered cafés by a wide margin. Just blocks from Times Square, you could find trash-strewn avenues lined with prostitutes—sometimes as many as 250 in a single night. Faced with the attendant drugs, violence, noise, and disorder at all hours, local residents and businesses were understandably up in arms. While many fled the area, those who stayed saw their property values plummet along with their sense of physical safety. According to Sue Cline, a local resident: "It was a diverse group of people who were just fed up. At the time I was [thinking] about starting a family, but how could I? The park by my home was littered with used condoms and anthills of crack vials."[2]

Residents weren't the only ones feeling the heat. The business community felt it too—none more so than the local theater industry. It didn't matter how good the shows were, the audience members (particularly those from out of town) voted with their feet, staying away in droves. The most vivid symbols of this phenomenon were the many theaters that simply stopped putting on shows, choosing to remain dark rather than risk failure.

But by the end of the decade, a very different story was being written in and around Times Square. In an article headlined "Hooker Haven No More," a local paper observed that "well-dressed twentysomethings" now dominated the neighborhood, "ordering coffee at trendy cafes."[3]

How did this transformation occur? As is always the case, success on this scale has many parents. Reams of newsprint have been devoted to the contributions made by former New York City mayor Rudy Giuliani, the New York Police Department, the Shubert Organization, the Walt Disney Corporation, the Times Square Business Improvement District, and others. One of the most unlikely and innovative partners in the clean-up of Times Square was the Midtown Community Court.

MIDTOWN COMMUNITY COURT

Located just blocks from Times Square, the Midtown Community Court was created in 1993 to focus exclusively on low-level crimes like prostitution, vandalism, and other forms of community disorder. According to Barbara Feldt, the founder of Residents Against Street Prostitution (RASP) and a long-time resident of midtown Manhattan, "[The Midtown Community Court is] the perfect link for the misdemeanor crime to be seen for what it truly is and what so many judges don't get— that there's a link between little crime and big crime."

The Midtown Community Court's approach marks a significant departure from standard operating practice. "Until the mid-1990s, New York City's prostitution enforcement policies were characterized by a deplorable lack of coordination between the police and the courts," writes researcher Robert Weidner.[4] Before Midtown, when residents complained loud and long enough, they would get some action: the cops swept the streets, making dozens of arrests in a single night. But after being arrested and processed back at the local precinct house, the prostitutes would be shuttled downtown and placed in the hands of judges in Manhattan's centralized courthouse. And that's where the system began to break down. According to Feldt, "The prostitutes were getting a free sandwich (in the downtown detention cells) and then were getting turned back out on the street. We actually watched the prostitutes with 'time-served' sentences leave the court and get into their pimps' cars, and we had to take the subway home. . . . They beat us back to the neighborhood and went right back to work."[5]

Residents like Feldt may have been the most graphic in expressing their disgust, but they weren't the only ones frustrated by the court system's response to prostitution. "We could make arrests," said Bruce Smolka of the New York City Police Department, "but there were no sentences for the people we arrested. It was a never-ending cycle."[6]

The Midtown Community Court was created to break the never-ending cycle by combining punishment and help. Defendants have no choice about whether their cases are heard at Midtown or not—anyone arrested for a misdemeanor crime within the three police precincts surrounding Times Square is automatically arraigned at Midtown. But once they arrive at Midtown, defendants do have a choice: they can either accept the alternative sanctions offered at Midtown or they can choose to fight their case in Manhattan's regular criminal court downtown.

Rather than being sentenced to "time served" or a few days in jail, low-level offenders at Midtown are by and large sentenced to repay the neighborhood they have harmed through visible restitution projects—sweeping the streets, painting over graffiti, cleaning local parks. For example, 86 percent of the prostitution cases that appear at the Court receive sentences of community restitution. Whenever possible, offenders begin their sanctions within twenty-four hours of seeing the judge. The idea here is twofold. By emphasizing immediacy, the Court ties a crime to its consequences. Just as important, immediacy helps reduce the chances that an offender will fail to appear—a familiar bugaboo for alternative-sanctions programs.

In fact, accountability is one of the recurring themes at the Midtown Community Court. Compliance with sanctions is closely monitored by the judge with the help of a computer tracking system. "It's a quick system," says Peppa, a prostitute sentenced at the Court. "It only takes about two or three hours to see a judge. And it's always a female judge. She's a bitch. I think she's harder on us because we're females like her. . . . Community service is all day—cleaning toilets and stuffing envelopes. . . . Even though I hate doing it, I guess the community service is fair."[7]

But punishment is just one side of the ledger at the Midtown Community Court. The other half of the equation is help. The Court houses an array of professional helpers on-site—counselors, educators, nurses, job trainers, and drug-treatment providers. They are there to address the problems—addiction, homelessness, unemployment—that are often associated with criminal behavior. The Midtown judge can mandate offenders to receive services, or they can take advantage of services voluntarily at any point in the process—even after they have completed their formal sanction at the Court.

While help is available for anyone who needs it, the Court tries not to take a one-size-fits-all approach to service delivery. For example, the Court has taken special pains to create social-service interventions targeted to the unique issues of prostitutes, many of whom suffer from drug abuse, domestic violence, low self-esteem, and other chronic problems. Prostitutes at the Midtown Community Court can participate in health education and counseling classes that help them understand the long-term risks of their behavior. At the same time, the Court's social workers work with each prostitute individually, impressing upon them the resources that are available if they are willing to make a commitment to get off the streets.

There is no denying that this approach is resource-intensive: the Midtown Community Court is home to a range of on-site services that simply don't exist in most criminal courts. Some government and nonprofit service providers agree to place staff at the court at no extra cost, recognizing that the Court can guarantee them thousands of clients each year. In other cases, the Court must pay for additional services to meet the needs of its defendants. In the project's first three years, these additional costs were born primarily by private funders. At the end of this "demonstration" period, local government assumed these costs, convinced by Midtown's results that it was an investment worth making.

The key to securing this ongoing funding was Midtown's ability to generate positive outcomes, both for the surrounding community and for individual offenders. Prostitutes provide the Court with perhaps its toughest challenge. Getting a prostitute out of the business is extremely complicated. Jeff Hobbs, a member of the Court's alternative-sanctions team, describes the process this way:

> Some of them eventually realize that the pimps just want their money, that love has nothing to do with it. We'll hear,

"He's not like other pimps," and then for some of them we'll stop hearing it and that's when we pounce. That's when engagement starts to work, and then the tears start to flow. . . . That's when the tag team begins. Everyone on the staff starts delivering the message: "I want you to know you can always come and see me. If you need a place to stay, I have a place for you." We've had pimps waiting in the courtroom while we've taken her down the back stairs and . . . gotten her on a bus going out of town.[8]

This common-sense approach—combining a message of accountability with a helping hand—has proven to be an effective one-two punch in Midtown. While the Court has not eliminated prostitution (it is, after all, the world's oldest profession), it has made a dramatic impact on the streets. According to independent evaluators, prostitution arrests dropped 56 percent after the Court opened.[9] Researcher Rob Weidner concluded, "The common perception among [prostitutes] was that it was a lot more difficult to work on Manhattan's streets, and that working conditions definitely had been affected by both enforcement efforts and . . . the sanctions of the Midtown Court."[10]

Researchers also documented the perception among neighborhood residents that the visible strolls had ground to a near halt, as many of the prostitutes remaining in the neighborhood chose to work indoors and by appointment. As a direct result of the community court, prostitution became less aggressive and less a daily feature of life on the streets of Midtown.

In May 1997, Feldt officially disbanded RASP, announcing that prostitution had been successfully eliminated from her neighborhood. "I felt comfortable saying good-bye to it and disbanding," Feldt says. "The prostitutes were no longer prostituting themselves for drugs. The police and the community had a good working relationship. The Court was up and running. All of a sudden there was no problem. We really did get rid of street prostitution."

Prostitution represents just a small percentage of the Midtown Community Court's daily calendar. The Court, which handles between ten and fifteen thousand cases each year, arraigns all misdemeanor offenses—illegal vending, low-level drug possession, disorderly conduct, shoplifting, vandalism, and the like—occurring in and around Times Square. These are precisely the kinds of offenses that many criminal courts label "victimless" crimes. True, there might not be an individual victim in a street-corner drug sale or a prostitution transaction, but these conditions assault the neighborhood on a daily basis, undermining the quality of life for the people who live and work in Midtown.

The Midtown Community Court's success in addressing quality-of-life crime has generated significant attention, both locally and nationally. Midtown has been the subject of numerous articles, television profiles, and conference panels. It has hosted hundreds of site visits from criminal justice officials around the country and has been promoted by the U.S. Department of Justice as a national model. In Midtown's wake have come dozens of other community courts, from Florida to California, each one seeking to adapt the model to the unique needs and problems of its host neighborhood. Perhaps no place has embraced the concept more wholeheartedly than Portland, Oregon.

PORTLAND, OREGON

While New York was the first city to invest in community courts, Portland was an early and enthusiastic adopter, opening its first community court in 1998. Since then, Portland has taken the idea citywide. It now handles all nonviolent misdemeanor crimes in the city in community court.

The key advocate for the community court idea in Portland was Michael Schrunk, the charismatic district attorney. According to Schrunk, "Courts can add a dimension to improving local neighborhoods by providing a consistent standard of response to quality-of-life offenses. . . . And, by locating the court in the affected communities, citizens feel a closer connection to their legal system and develop a greater appreciation of how the rule of law can . . . make their neighborhoods safer."[11]

Schrunk's advocacy was crucial to the success of the community court idea in Portland. One of the most influential political voices in the city, Schrunk has served as district attorney since 1981. But Schrunk's roots go deeper than that. His office is located just a few steps from Schrunk Plaza, a memorial to his father, the former mayor of Portland. By throwing the weight of his office behind the project, he was able to attract federal money, bring the other necessary institutional players (judges, defenders, police) to the table, and garner favorable media attention. Schrunk even helped to draft the project's mission statement:

> The Community Court Project endeavors to address quality-of-life crime that diminishes citizens' pride and sense of safety in their neighborhoods. By collaborating with citizens, law enforcement, court and social service agencies, the Community Court Project encourages defendants to contribute positively to their community through community service projects and offers them social service assistance to address underlying problems that can lead to criminal behavior.

How well does Portland live up to these ideals? A trip to the Community Court in Southeast, a working-class neighborhood of modest one-story bungalows, offers some answers.

A DELICATE BALANCING ACT

The defendant, a slight Hispanic man speaking through an interpreter, can barely suppress a smile as he struggles to answer the judge's seemingly obvious question: Why did he approach a prostitute to inquire about the prices of various sex acts? He's appearing at the Community Court, which meets one day each week in a local community center.

Today's makeshift courtroom has a decidedly grassroots atmosphere. The prosecutor and defense attorney stand at folding metal cafeteria tables, and children playing in the adjacent school yard are visible through the windows. But the manner of the judge could not be more serious.

Unfortunately for the defendant, the prostitute he approached on Eighty-second Street, a neighborhood street notorious for prostitution, was an undercover cop. The man, who lives on the other side of the city, has pled guilty, admitting that he approached the prostitute. His reason? In his own words, "foolishness."

But the judge won't let it go at that. "Do you have any idea why what you did is illegal in this community?" asks Judge Clifford L. Freeman in a voice that carries easily to the back of the courtroom, where a handful of other defendants and local residents are watching from molded plastic chairs.

"I don't know," the defendant replies, bewildered by the attention the judge is giving this minor infraction.

"Most people know there's prostitution around Eighty-second Street. But there are also people who live around Eighty-second Street," says Judge Freeman, leaning forward.

"In the afternoon and evenings, when children are on their way to the store or a friend's house or after-school activities, they get men rolling up to them saying 'Hey, baby; hey *chica*, are you working? Want to come with me?' It's degrading and demeaning. I don't think you'd want anyone to do that to your wife or daughter. And the people who live out here don't want it happening either. They don't want you to give their community a reputation where those things are permitted."

Judge Freeman goes on to draw a picture of the dire repercussions this minor crime could have on the defendant's family. "You could expose your wife to disease," he adds. "If you contract HIV, you could die—just for the reason that you wanted to get a smile on your face coming home from work. It could result in your child being an orphan."

By now, Judge Freeman has spent close to twenty minutes on a charge that would receive the scantest of attention in most big-city courts. The judge closes by sentencing the man to twenty-four hours of community service and a stay-away order excluding him from the area where the incident occurred. If the defendant fails to complete the community service, the judge informs him, he faces jail time.

Later, in his chambers, Judge Freeman explains that he engages in such lengthy colloquies primarily for the benefit of the defendant—to get the person to reflect on the repercussions of the offense in hopes of changing future behavior. But the judge's lecture is also a form of public theater aimed at the broader audience in the courtroom and the community at large, he explains. He is sending a signal to residents that the court values the area's quality of life and that infractions won't be tolerated.

Many people consider prostitution relatively benign, Freeman acknowledges, and that's another reason he spends so much time explaining the potentially damaging conse-

quences. Freeman has seen its degrading effects on a neighborhood firsthand. Growing up in Northeast Portland, home
to the city's largest concentration of African Americans, he
has vivid memories of women friends and co-workers being
accosted by would-be "johns" from the other side of town.
Judge Freeman tries to disabuse offenders of the notion that
solicitation is okay as long as it's in someone else's neighborhood. "From the standpoint of the community court, the
notion is that we all have interdependent relations," no matter what neighborhood we're from, he stresses.

As Freeman's stern lecture indicates, community courts
sometimes come across as "hard on crime"—especially for
minor infractions that would get little attention in a conventional court. Portland residents who are active in the
city's community courts say that the public admonition in
front of neighborhood residents is extremely important.
"Because most defendants are from Southeast, this is a way
of making them accountable to the neighborhood. They
have to stand in front of their peers from this neighborhood," says Dick Hazeltine, a retired electrician and lifelong
resident who sits on the community court's advisory board
and spends every Thursday observing court in session.

Richard Brown, president of the Black United Front, agrees
that Portland's community courts make offenders take seriously infractions that were once ignored by the police and
the courts. "We put you in the middle of the town square and
say 'You all come and watch this.' " Brown is a regular fixture
at community court, and he makes a point of greeting neighbors who have been charged with an offense. "I come to court
so I can remind you that I know you," he says.

For all of the tough talk from the judge and local residents, public defenders say they support the community
court primarily because they see it as a better deal for their

clients: a defendant charged with a first offense who completes the court's community service mandate will have the charges wiped out and will emerge with no criminal record. Prosecutors say they support the community court's emphasis on mandating services, like drug treatment, because it makes it less likely that a person will steal again to support a habit. It's a delicate balancing act, communicating a message of zero tolerance and second chances simultaneously.

"THE SMALL PETTY STUFF"

How did this agenda emerge? The story begins back in the 1980s. At the time, Richard Brown's neighborhood, Northeast, was plagued with gang-related shootings. He remembers one elderly resident who slept in the bathtub to avoid being hit by a stray bullet. Bob Lockwood, a professor at Portland State University and a twenty-year resident of the neighborhood, can recall gang members stopping their cars in front of his house on a Sunday afternoon to carry out a gunfight. The sounds of police sirens regularly punctuated the night. By the early 1990s, the violence had declined, but the low-income neighborhood continued to be plagued with prostitution, drug use, vandalism, and graffiti. Residents were frustrated by the lack of attention to these minor crimes from the police and the courts. Recalls Lockwood, "In poor areas and the minority area where I lived, the feeling was, 'Unless someone's shooting at you, you won't get much of a response.' "

It was a message Portland district attorney Mike Schrunk had been hearing for some time. In 1994, Schrunk visited Manhattan's newly opened Midtown Community Court and became intrigued with developing a similar court in Portland. Community courts looked to Schrunk like a logical progression from a community prosecution program he had started in 1990. Shortly after he was first elected, Schrunk raised enough money to give downtown Portland a special prosecutor who focused exclusively on the petty offenses that were undermining the neighborhood. Neighborhood groups around the city called the prosecutor's office, asking, "Can we get a prosecutor too?" Schrunk recalls.

Recognizing an unmet need, Schrunk started expanding the local-prosecutor program to all residential neighborhoods. As part of their new job, the local prosecutors attended neighborhood meetings to hear firsthand what problems were of greatest concern to residents. What they learned was that quality-of-life crimes mattered as much as violent crime. As a prosecutor, says Schrunk, "You tend to blow off" crimes like vandalism, turnstile jumping, petty shoplifting, and prostitution because they're "not as important as rape and robbery. . . . But what really drives people out of a neighborhood or makes a neighborhood rot from the inner core is the small, petty stuff."

Just as broken-windows and problem-oriented policing had started to change the philosophy of the police, community prosecution programs like Schrunk's gave prosecutors an increasingly local orientation. But when they got to court, they weren't finding much of a response from judges. Petty crimes tended to drag on for months in Portland's court system without resolution. Judges overburdened with heavy dockets and cases involving more serious crimes had little time to deal with less weighty neighborhood offenses. If the defendant showed up in court, "It just became part of the culture [for the judge to say], 'Well, they're here; that's punishment enough,'" Schrunk recalls.

At most, petty offenders were put on "bench probation," a form of probation with few conditions and next to no oversight. At community meetings, local residents increasingly told Schrunk they were dissatisfied with the centralized downtown court system, which they saw as insensitive to their concerns.

Over the years, in an effort to change sentencing practices for petty crimes, Schrunk had organized citizen letter-writing campaigns to judges and had even chartered buses of concerned citizens to the courts—all to no avail. His visit to the Midtown Community Court made him realize that a local court could be an innovative way to change the standard practice of judges. He liked the idea of having offenders pay back the community by working on constructive neighborhood projects. But above all, he says, "I liked the immediacy of the sentencing"—the way offenders were scheduled for community-service assignments and mandated social services immediately after appearing in court. In Portland, even when petty offenders received community service sentences, they rarely showed up.

Schrunk started floating the idea of a community court at meetings of citizen groups. "What surprised us was that the idea immediately resonated with people," recalls Schrunk's staff assistant, Judy Phelan. Initially, the project faced skepticism from the city's police, who viewed community service as too light a punishment. Judges also were resistant to any change in their traditional practice. But the project gathered steam over a four-year period, as Schrunk used his political influence and enthusiasm to build support among crucial players like public defenders and community leaders.

The turning point came when Schrunk took the court's presiding judge, whose sign-off was crucial, to visit the Midtown Community Court. The presiding judge became an advocate after he saw with his own eyes the difference a community court could make. Schrunk also secured federal funding to jump-start the court in its first three years of operation.

On March 4, 1998, Portland opened its first community court in Northeast, at a community center next to a grade school. The court handles nonviolent misdemeanors and code violations including excessive noise, chronic housing-code violations, and solicitation of prostitutes. Community service is the primary sanction imposed in exchange for a guilty plea from the defendant. Other sanctions may include writing an essay or attendance at a "theft deterrent" class aimed at helping defendants understand how shoplifting hurts their community. In most cases, alternative sanctions are backed up by a jail sentence if the defendant fails to comply. Under sentencing guidelines developed with the help of neighborhood residents, mandated community service hours increase with each subsequent offense—as do the number of days in jail for failing to complete community service.

DOES IT WORK?

Has the court succeeded in reducing crime in the Northeast neighborhood? Anecdotally, residents report there is less prostitution and trash in the neighborhood. Daytime shootings are a thing of the past. According to unpublished data collected by John Roman of the Urban Institute, crime in the neighborhood became more dispersed after the court opened. There were fewer hot spots—corners or blocks where crime is concentrated—and the remaining troubled areas had less crime. In addition, after the court went into operation, there was a significant decrease in the number of calls to the police for service, according to Roman, suggesting the court was actually having an impact on crime.[12]

With the opening of the community courts, "The police have an avenue to start enforcing these laws again," says Schrunk of the quality-of-life offenses that once went ignored. In addition, a higher proportion of offenders appear for their court dates in community courts than in the old centralized downtown court, according to Schrunk's office. One reason may simply be that most offenders find it easier to get to the neighborhood-based courts. Another may be that police are more likely to pick up offenders who have failed to appear. "The police now know that something can happen in court, so they're more vigilant," says Schrunk. "They know when John Doe is out wandering around and should be in court. So they bring him in."

Portland's community courts have also managed to prod notoriously unresponsive landlords into bringing dilapidated buildings up to code. Unsightly run-down buildings were among the top quality-of-life concerns cited by neighborhood residents. Since local prosecutors started taking property owners with code violations to court, the number of code-compliant properties has risen, and the number of repeat violators has declined.[13]

Yet as with all reductions in crime or improvements in neighborhood quality of life, it's hard to know how much to attribute to the community court. The opening of the community court in Northeast coincided with other significant changes in the neighborhood. The nineties saw young professional couples move in, attracted by the low home prices and the proximity to downtown. Alberta Avenue, where prostitutes once strolled and the drug trade and vandalism thrived in abandoned buildings, is now dotted with trendy restaurants, galleries, and outdoor cafés.

The city also beefed up police patrols and instituted "drug-free zones," which permitted the courts to exclude low-level drug offenders from neighborhoods where they bought or sold drugs. "Now the violence is significantly less and the trash is also significantly less," says Portland State

University professor Bob Lockwood, a veteran Northeast resident. "And I think the community court probably played a role in it. It was one of many things that helped."

As an example of community court success, Richard Brown points to Dawson Park, a neighborhood park once so dominated by drunks that families did not feel safe using it. "For a long time, someone had to be really obnoxious to be stopped [by the police] with an open container of alcohol," he says. As a result, the neighborhood was skeptical about the willingness of police to get things under control. Through a combination of community pressure and collaboration between the police and community court, officers started giving out tickets for public drinking in the park. "Now you see kids at the swings, playing basketball, people playing dominoes and cards," Brown reports.

THE RED HOOK COMMUNITY JUSTICE CENTER

Portland's story raises an interesting question: Can reductions in crime and fear spur a neighborhood's economic development?

This question is being posed in earnest in Red Hook, Brooklyn. Red Hook is a neighborhood with the twin burdens of being physically isolated (it is surrounded on three sides by water and cut off from the rest of Brooklyn by an elevated expressway) and having a dismal reputation for drugs and disorder. In the early 1990s, some Red Hook residents were so fed up with the public perception of their neighborhood that they tried to change the name to "Liberty Heights." Like so much in Red Hook, this effort never gathered much momentum and ultimately failed.

But Red Hook's reputation for crime and dysfunction is only part of the story. Spend a day in the neighborhood and you'll find an expansive waterfront with beautiful views of the Statue of Liberty. You'll see tree-lined parks, soccer fields, and baseball diamonds. And you'll meet great people—families who have lived there for several generations, leaders who are utterly devoted to their neighborhood, shopkeepers who know their customers by name.

Red Hook is perhaps the epitome of a neighborhood that, if it could just wrestle its public-safety problems under control, would be a truly pleasant place to live. Just ask Emma Broughton, a diminutive, energetic seventy-four-year-old widow who is known informally as the Mayor of Red Hook. Walking through the streets of Red Hook, Broughton is recognized by practically everyone, and most people greet her with a hug. In fact, anyone who wants to get anything done in Red Hook is instructed to "Meet Miss Emma."

Emma Broughton has earned that reputation because of her efforts to make Red Hook a better place to raise children. As a mother, she is intimately familiar with the difficulties of raising a family in the midst of drug dealing and gunplay. She has lived in Red Hook for forty-four years and raised five children in the neighborhood.

In the lilting tones of her native North Carolina, Broughton tells the depressing story of a neighborhood's seemingly inexorable decline, from the good old days in the 1950s, when longshoremen worked along the neighborhood's waterfront, to the dire 1980s, when commercial shipping abandoned Red Hook for the more modern facilities and easier access to highways offered by New Jersey. She still mourns the shops that moved out with the jobs, leaving Red Hook isolated and without a decent grocery store.

During the crack epidemic of the 1980s, the turf battles over Red Hook's drug markets turned the neighborhood into a "war zone" in Miss Emma's words. "People were afraid to go out of their houses. They were afraid to look out the window because of the constant shooting," she remembers. Indeed, the poor aim of young dealers fighting over turf earned them the moniker the "Can't Shoot Straight Gang."

THE CAN'T SHOOT STRAIGHT GANG

The Can't Shoot Straight Gang was strictly a neighborhood concern until 1992, when Patrick Daly, a popular elementary-school principal, was slain by a stray bullet from a shoot-out between rival drug dealers. Daly had left school property to search for a truant student. "He loved his children," recalls Broughton. "He would be the first person in the morning to make sure the kids got on the school grounds safe and the last one to leave."

Daly's death shone a highly unflattering spotlight on Red Hook. Long a forgotten neighborhood in New York City, Red Hook found itself the subject of hand-wringing editorials and concerned city officials. One such official was Brooklyn's district attorney, Charles J. Hynes, who publicly called for the creation of a community court in Red Hook to help address crime and disorder in the neighborhood.

In a recent interview, Hynes recalled the anger and frustration he encountered in Red Hook after Daly's death. "I went to [Daly's] wake and the funeral, and I spoke to a lot of people, and they kept telling me, 'You don't care about us. We got cut off years ago, with that horrible monstrosity [the elevated Gowanus Expressway] that divided us from the city.' "[14]

Hynes wasn't the only public official who thought a community court for Red Hook was a good idea. By the middle of 1994, New York State Chief Judge Judith Kaye had taken up the cause as well.

Emma Broughton was one of the first residents contacted when the prospect of a community court was on the drawing board. As Miss Emma remembers it, most of the neighborhood residents who participated in the planning process through focus groups, interviews, and town hall meetings agreed that their number-one problem was drug use and all that came with it. "Drug dealers was really messing up the area; they were outside all day and night," Broughton recalls. "They would litter. They would do graffiti in the buildings. They were doing damage to the buildings, breaking windows. You couldn't keep a door locked. They'd break the locks on the doors."

As Broughton remembers it, most of the residents said they wanted "a cleaner community." For example, many residents said they were afraid to go into Coffey Park, at the center of Red Hook, because the benches were occupied by drug dealers and the grass was littered with broken glass.

At the organizing meetings, there were always a handful of naysayers—residents who were worried that putting a court in the neighborhood would bring in more criminals or too much traffic. Some residents in the predominantly minority neighborhood expressed suspicion of any institution connected to the criminal justice system. District Attorney Hynes acknowledges this reality. "If you speak to people of color in this county," he says, "they will tell you that when justice moved downtown, they became suspicious of it. You've got to break down that suspicion. You've got to have people see what a justice program looks like."[15]

Although she understood the concerns, Broughton still chose to advocate for the community court: "I felt if we'd had something like the community court, the neighborhood would never have gotten to the point it was."

Over time, thanks to the input of Broughton and other residents, a vision for Red Hook began to emerge that would bring the resources of the court system to bear on a host of neighborhood problems, including drugs, disorder, domestic violence, and delinquency. Crucially, the court would provide services not just to offenders, but to everyone touched by crime in Red Hook—defendants, victims, and those in the community who were simply worried about safety. Recognizing the unique nature of the project, the court system decided to call the project a "community justice center," signifying their intention to build much more than just a courtroom in Red Hook.

"A WARM, FRIENDLY PLACE"

The Red Hook Community Justice Center opened its doors in 2000 in a refurbished parochial school that had been empty for twenty years—a powerful symbol of Red Hook's decline. As Broughton had hoped, many residents who have no involvement with the criminal justice system take advantage of services at the Justice Center. Her grandson, for example, got his GED through the Center, which offers classes at night. An elderly friend of Broughton's recently found an apartment by seeking help from the court's housing specialists, even though she wasn't involved in a court case. As word of mouth has traveled, some residents have gone so far as to seek voluntary drug treatment at the Justice Center.

According to Broughton, these are just a few signs that the Justice Center has set a new tone in Red Hook. "Residents can relate to it because it's such a warm friendly place to walk into," she says. Even Red Hook's court officers have entered into the spirit. Some tutor children after school. Others coach in the court's youth baseball league during the summer. "The court officers reach out. They know the kids and the kids know the court officers," according to Broughton.

Court officers aren't the only ones who make a special effort. Red Hook's presiding judge, Alex Calabrese, can often be seen out on the ball field playing with local kids. According to Calabrese, "As a judge in a traditional court, I felt like an artist with two colors: in jail or out of jail. . . . At the Justice Center, I have the tools to give people the opportunity to change their lives. Not everyone is successful, but the Justice Center provides defendants with the structure and support they need to avoid being arrested again and again. After all, don't people deserve a real chance to change their lives before they are locked up? . . . The Justice Center has changed the life trajectories of hundreds of people for the better. How many courts can say that?"

As Broughton points out, the people who are brought before the judge are not only defendants—many are also the sons and daughters of neighbors she knows. From her perspective, the community has an interest in making sure they complete mandated drug treatment or counseling. At the same time, she appreciates Calabrese's no-nonsense reputation. If a defendant doesn't carry out an alternative sentence, the judge "will give them time. People know that," she says.

Today, Emma Broughton is no longer the only senior citizen in Red Hook who feels safe enough to venture out of her apartment. In 2004, for the first time in a generation, Red Hook went an entire calendar year without a homicide. Door-to-door surveys reveal that the number of Red Hook residents who say they feel unsafe has steadily declined since the Justice Center opened. As Broughton puts it, the law-abiding "eyes of the community" have begun to reclaim the streets of Red Hook.

PERCEPTION VERSUS REALITY

Organizers of community courts have found that the perception of safety in a neighborhood is almost as important
as the reality, especially when it comes to investment decisions like buying a home or a business. Mike Schrunk is convinced that residents' changing perceptions of Portland's
Northeast neighborhood from a drug- and crime-ridden
ghetto to a safe neighborhood has contributed to its economic vibrancy. "What's it worth to have people patronize
restaurants in Northeast Portland in the evening after
dark?" he asks. That feeling of safety, he argues, can make
the difference between an economically healthy neighborhood and a blighted community abandoned by shopkeepers
moving to distant suburban malls, by middle-class residents
moving to gated communities, and by parents afraid to send
their kids to the local public schools.

Susan Cox, a long-time resident of Southeast Portland,
agrees with Schrunk's analysis. According to Cox, before the
arrival of community court, the area had become so unlivable that she and her husband contemplated leaving—even
though houses there were affordable and the couple desperately wanted to own their own home. Local police routinely told residents they were so overburdened with crime
calls that they couldn't respond to complaints of public
drinking, loitering, and graffiti. "Yet these were the things
that add up, giving the neighborhood a bad reputation, and
making everyday life unbearable," Cox recalled.[16]

Things have changed since the opening of the community court. According to Cox, "Now people are buying property, and when you own property, you care about it. It's hard
to believe this is the same area it was just a few years ago.
Now we feel like we can really invest in a home here."[17]

OPENING THE COURTHOUSE DOORS

Perhaps the most important goal of community courts is to address the alienation from the justice system that citizens—especially in poor and minority neighborhoods—often feel.

Bob Lockwood, who participated in numerous community meetings prior to the founding of Portland's community courts, says, "There wasn't a real sense . . . in the community that [the justice system] really cared. [People wanted to know that] if someone messed up a building, spilled trash, or blasted their stereo at an incredible volume, the system would respond and people would have to recognize some responsibility to the community. . . . One of the main concerns was to focus on addressing the community's sense of alienation. By giving someone jail time or probation or a fine, you really didn't do anything to clean up the graffiti, the streets, or the park."

As Lockwood makes clear, Portland residents view community service as far more than make-work. Elderly residents have attended community-court celebrations to express their appreciation for supervised offender work crews that perform yard work—a program available to any resident age sixty and over on a fixed income.[18] Offenders have also cleaned parks and bike trails, painted over graffiti, landscaped the local public school grounds, planted vegetables at a local community garden, and prepared Red Cross blood bags for donations.

Portland's community courts have improved compliance with community-service sentences by making it hard to avoid. Sixty percent of offenders complete their community service sentences. The comparable figure for misdemeanors handled in Portland's downtown central court is about 40 percent, according to the district attorney's office.[19] In the regular downtown court, defendants have to go to a separate office to schedule their community service—which means they often don't make it there. By contrast, immediately after receiving a sentence in community court, each defendant meets at a courtroom table with a court staff person to schedule the mandated work. This increased sense of accountability has helped local residents feel comfortable with the idea of offenders performing community service on their streets.

Indeed, the atmosphere generated by today's community courts in Portland, the sense of connection between the court and local residents, could not be more apparent. Strikingly, local activist Richard Brown uses the term "we" when discussing community court. As the court has evolved, Brown and other residents have served on the project's advisory board, which includes representatives of the court, prosecutors, and defenders. They help decide what kinds of social services should be available in the courtroom and are asked to offer new ideas for community-service projects. The court staff and attorneys, Brown says, "make citizens feel like they are part of the process. Nothing happens here that doesn't go through the advisory board."

Not long ago, the advisory board of the Northeast community court held its monthly Wednesday-evening meeting at a local recreation center. The meeting took place under the watchful eyes of Martin Luther King Jr., staring down from an oil portrait and a banner reading, "Injustice anywhere is a threat to justice everywhere." Community residents sat at a table that included Judge Freeman, a local police officer, and representatives of the district attorney's office and the public defender's office.

Residents at the meeting complained that judges were being too easy on offenders who failed to complete their mandated community service, giving them numerous chances to complete the community service rather than promptly imposing a jail sentence. One resident argued that defendants were starting to count on the judges' leniency and weren't taking the community-service mandate seriously. She approvingly cited the case of a repeat offender who had finally been slapped with a jail sentence. "I think she was impressed because she thought she would get out of it again," she said.

None of the criminal justice officials at the table got defensive or argued the point. The meeting's collaborative atmosphere was a striking departure from the usual courtroom roles. In a conventional situation, the prosecutor, rather than a community resident, could have been expected to lead the charge for tougher sentencing practices. And the public defender could normally have been expected to protest any crackdown. Instead, the prosecutor and the defender did their job that evening by listening to the voices of residents instead of talking. The meeting closed with an agreement that the group would draw up a set of recommendations for judges on dealing with community-service laggards, with the understanding that the ultimate authority to determine sentencing would still lie with the judge.

The community court's practice of opening its doors to the community and making partners of traditional outsiders is a distinctive trait of problem-solving courts. Drug courts rely heavily on progress reports from substance-abuse treatment counselors in deciding whether to sanction or graduate a defendant. And domestic-violence courts consult frequently with batterers' intervention programs to determine if a defendant is complying with court orders, or if the orders need to be changed.

CHANGING ROLES

The Northeast community court advisory board's meeting illustrates one of the most challenging demands of problem-solving courts: a shift in the traditional roles of courtroom players. Defenders, who are accustomed to battling prosecutors to get the best deal for their clients, are often asked to work alongside them as part of a collaborative team. These cooperative efforts often start on the ground floor with traditional adversaries working together to design guidelines, eligibility criteria, and sanctioning schemes. When a drug-court judge hands down a three-day jail sentence because an addict has failed to attend his treatment program, defenders are often surprisingly silent, because they—and their clients—have already accepted the idea of intermediate jail sanctions as part of the treatment sentence.

Prosecutors, too, play different roles. In Portland, prosecutors attend neighborhood meetings to get the pulse of the community and to gather intelligence on trouble spots. Rather than waiting for a crime to be committed and an arrestee to show up in court, prosecutors take an active role in preventing problems. For example, when the Northeast community court received a rash of underage drinking cases and complaints about loud parties coming from an area close to a local college, a prosecutor went to talk to the college about the problems. To Richard Brown, "It's been a great example of how something caught the attention of community courts" that in ordinary circumstances would probably have been invisible to criminal justice officials downtown. It is also an example of prosecutors responding to a problem with a solution that doesn't rest exclusively on enforcement and prosecution.

Judges take on new roles too. In problem-solving courts, the judge is often the leader of a team composed of defenders, prosecutors, and clinical staff, which must respond as a unit when an offender relapses into drug use. Judges may find themselves taking a leadership role outside of the courtroom as well as within—for example, convening local agencies in an attempt to prod them into providing much-needed services to court participants. It is not unusual for a problem-solving court judge to make phone calls to local service providers to find a bed for an addicted parent or to cut through the red tape tying up a client's health insurance.

Like Judge Freeman, many problem-solving judges engage in direct colloquies with defendants. This is a stark departure from conventional criminal courts, where judges tend to rely upon defense lawyers to be a defendant's mouthpiece. Drug-court judges often clap for defendants who have successfully completed treatment. Public defenders, who would normally object to a client's revealing any extraneous personal information, are apt to accept these conversations, knowing that encouraging words from an authority figure like the judge can be extremely helpful to a client struggling to achieve sobriety.

ADDRESSING PROBLEMS

"You don't want to stamp the defendants as criminals forever," says Mike Schrunk. "Some are people in unfortunate circumstances driven to do this stuff." According to Schrunk, "We started looking at this population and realized they needed a whole array of services." As a result, many community-court offenders receive not only a sanction for their offense but also access to drug treatment, health care, job training, and other services designed to address their underlying problems.

A day in any one of Portland's community courts finds the judge inquiring with concern about the reasons each defendant has landed in court. The answers typically include a litany of personal problems—homelessness, poverty,

hunger, drug use. About half the cases that come to Portland's community courts have drug or alcohol abuse at
their root, according to Heidi Grant, a clinical psychologist
who interviews defendants before they appear in court.
Many of the defendants suffer from undiagnosed mental
illnesses. In some cases, the court's mandate linking a
defendant to treatment may be the first time their mental
illness has been treated.

Community courts attempt to tackle offenders' problems
by linking them to services on both a mandated and voluntary basis. New York's community courts have sophisticated
computer systems to aid in this process. Interviewers enter
information into a computer about each defendant's housing situation, job status, education, and drug use. The presiding judge can see this information on a computer at the
bench before entering into a conversation with the defendant and setting a sentence.

Sometimes a perceptive judge can elicit valuable information that can aid social-service interventions. For example, Freeman cites several cases of women who were
brought into community court on shoplifting charges. Each
of them turned out to be going through a difficult divorce
or marriage. He was able to refer them to counseling and
give them the opportunity to wipe the charges from their
record if they completed community service. Under a more
conventional court scenario, a judge would never have
bothered to inquire about this kind of information. And the
options at the judge's disposal might have been limited to
jail, probation, or a fine.

Some defendants are struck by how differently they are
treated in community court. In a recent letter to Portland's
Westside community court, a defendant who had gone into
drug treatment after entering the court wrote, "Judge, I

want to say that you saw in me what most people have over-looked and you taught me that not every [judge] reads what's on the paper and expects the worst. You actually saw the hurt and pain in my eyes and wanted to help."

Victoria, a former heroin addict, was homeless and using a cocktail of illegal drugs when she was arrested for shoplifting a coat from a downtown Portland department store. A month after her court date, she was clean of illegal drugs and serving her community service by assisting the court clerk every day. She now has housing and plans to take classes to complete her GED. "Everyone in here has been terribly kind and made me feel better about myself," she says.

Watching community court judge Steve Todd in Portland, no one would find it difficult to understand why a defendant would be grateful. When the judge asks defendants why they committed a particular offense, he acts genuinely concerned. When he assigns them to write an essay about what they have learned from coming to court, he has the tone of a helpful English teacher who wants them to consider the subject thoughtfully. He is generous with praise when a defendant returns with a well-written essay.

"In the regular courtroom, people are abused by judges," Todd says. "We've gotten into such volume [in the court system], we don't slow down," to ask questions of the defendant or even make eye contact, he says. "Defendants think nobody cares. If nobody's paying attention to my behavior, why should I change it?" By contrast, says Todd, "I actually listen to them and say, 'Why are you doing this?' "

The defendants who appear in community court may not have complicated legal problems, but they do have complicated lives. In the course of one morning at Southeast community court, for example, Judge Freeman finds out that a man pleading guilty to shoplifting $100 worth of aspirin with the intention of reselling it has been unemployed for eight months. The man tells the judge he needed the money for food and school supplies for his girlfriend's daughter. The judge refers the man to a job-training program and a program that distributes emergency food.

A young woman who pleads guilty to stealing food from a grocery store says she is unemployed and lacks the money to buy food for herself and her son. She hid the food in her young son's backpack exiting the store. As the judge lectures her about exposing her son to the trauma of arrest by making him an unwitting mule, the woman is reduced to tears. He refers her to a family counseling center.

Intriguingly, residents active in Portland's community courts are just as likely to cite the courts' success in helping individuals as they are to mention any immediate visible impact on their neighborhoods. "I look at individuals," says Brown. "If you stop them from doing what they're doing, the community is better off." He is more supportive of services like drug treatment than of jail, because offenders "go in [to jail] thieves and they come out thieves." Brown cites the case of an elderly alcoholic who was sent by the court into a detoxification program. After the man got his act together, the court arranged for him to get into a senior citizens' home. "He's off the streets," says Brown with satisfaction.

Similarly, Southeast resident Dick Hazeltine says that as a result of the personal time defendants get with the judge and the social services they receive, "a lot of people report it made a difference in their lives." He cites the case of a woman defendant who showed up in court with a black eye. The judge asked about the injury and referred the woman to domestic-violence services. "To me that's impressive—he might be saving the woman's life," Hazeltine said.

RIGOROUS JUDICIAL MONITORING

Of course, linking someone to services is one thing—making sure she takes advantage is another challenge entirely. In the past, courts have often been reluctant to help defendants access help, because there was little guarantee that they would actually perform the services as ordered.[20]

In an effort to meet this challenge, most problem-solving courts rely on intensive judicial monitoring. In Portland's community courts, for example, offenders diagnosed with addiction problems are typically mandated to attend a drug program and required to return to court at least once a month so the court can monitor their attendance and test for drugs. The court's psychologist keeps tabs by contacting the offender's treatment counselors frequently by phone. A defendant's failure to comply can earn him a sanction of up to five days in jail. "It's a small stick, but it's immediate," says Judge Todd.

By contrast, a judge who orders an offender to attend drug treatment in Portland's conventional court usually has to rely on a probation officer to enforce attendance. The city's probation officers are so burdened with enormous caseloads that making contact with a probationer is infrequent at best, and contact with a treatment program is unlikely. Feedback to the sentencing judge almost never happens. "On probation, it could take months or years before [the offender] gets picked up" for violating a treatment mandate, Todd notes.

This emphasis on treatment, backed by stringent monitoring, is at the heart of the problem-solving model. Drug courts have shown that court-mandated offenders are twice as likely to stay in treatment as those who seek help voluntarily. For judicial monitoring to be effective, most judges agree, two elements are essential: information and immediacy. At the Brooklyn Treatment Court, a drug court in New York, participants return to court at least monthly for drug testing and appearances before the judge, who has an array of sanctions and rewards at her disposal to encourage compliance. The judge's ability to respond swiftly with a sanction to a participant who has resumed drug use or committed another crime is made possible because the information is available on her computer screen at the push of a button.

Of course, swiftness is the antithesis of the experience most drug-abusing offenders have with the conventional criminal justice system, observes Brooklyn Treatment Court judge Jo Ann Ferdinand. In the conventional system, she points out, "If you're arrested today on an additional drug charge, you have consequences months and months later. This is the same lesson addicts have to unlearn," she notes, because they live in the present, telling themselves in effect, "I won't use the drug—until next time."

Even more so than drug court or community court, aggressive judicial monitoring is crucial to the success of domestic-violence courts. Experience indicates that domestic-violence victims are particularly vulnerable while a case is pending and their accused batterer is out on bail. Recognizing this, domestic-violence courts typically require defendants to attend batterers' intervention programs as a condition of release. While there is considerable debate over the ability of such programs to change a batterer's behavior, at the very least domestic-violence courts have found that these programs are an effective way to monitor defendants when they are at their greatest risk of reoffending. Defendants must return to court to demonstrate that they are participating as required. Failure to attend can result in a jail sentence. "The defendant now knows someone is watching them constantly, knows this is not lawful conduct, and knows it is behavior the courts will not tolerate," says Scott Kessler, bureau chief of the district attorney's domestic-violence bureau in Queens, New York. "It has helped victim safety for sure."

INFORMED DECISIONS

In a community court, the stakes may be lower and the crimes less serious, but the value of an engaged, watchful judge is no less meaningful.

On a typical morning at the Midtown Community Court in New York City, several young women have been brought in for prostitution. For the first case—a redhead dressed in a low-cut fringed jersey—the computer screen indicates it is her first arrest for prostitution. After the woman pleads guilty, Judge Eileen Koretz sentences her to one day of community service and a session of health education—part of the court's efforts to make prostitutes face up to the dangers and risks of their lifestyle.

The next prostitution case gets much harsher treatment from Judge Koretz. The wan young woman in a revealing, open-cut white lace blouse has given her age as twenty, but she looks barely eighteen. On the computer screen before the judge, a flashing icon reads "persistent misdemeanor," alerting the judge to the defendant's lengthy criminal record. She has been to the court for the same charge already four times, the computer screen informs Judge Koretz, who recognizes her from the previous appearances. The young woman is prepared to plead guilty, and her lawyer promises her client will complete community service—as she did each previous time before the community court.

"She's run out of chances here," says Judge Koretz. She sentences the defendant to thirty days in jail.

Koretz's familiarity with persistent offenders gives her a chance to be strategic, making more informed decisions about when, where, and how to come down hard on an individual offender. This stands in stark contrast to the judges downtown, processing thousands of cases in multiple courtrooms.

"Downtown, the attitude is 'Oh yeah, she's a prostitute. It's a victimless crime,'" says Koretz. Residents have long complained that prostitutes get off with "time served" downtown and are back working the streets the same day. "Here, by contrast, we'll try to help them," says Koretz. "But when I've been trying to help them and they keep prostituting, I have no problem putting them in jail." The statistics back her up. Evaluators found that the Midtown Community Court dispenses fewer jail sentences than comparable criminal courts, but that when the Midtown judge does impose jail, it tends to be for longer sentences.[21]

At the end of the day, whether it's Portland, Midtown, Red Hook, or some place else, the success or failure of community courts will depend upon their ability to address or ameliorate neighborhood problems like prostitution, drugs, and disorder. In a low-income neighborhood like Red Hook, a community court is not going to be a panacea. But residents there give the Red Hook Community Justice Center credit for making it possible to carry out many of the activities middle-class people take for granted, such as sending their children outside to play or taking a stroll on a sunny afternoon.

Emma Broughton remembers when the housing project's play area was deserted, despite the presence of sprinklers that had been installed for the pleasure of neighborhood children. "On a hot summer day you'd walk through the play area and you wouldn't see a kid in the sprinkler. That tells you something. The parents were too afraid to let the kids out," Broughton recalls.

Today, she credits the Red Hook community court for reducing the open drug use and associated violence. Just as important to her have been the court's efforts to sentence low-level offenders to clean up play areas and local parks once littered with glass. With the court's help, these public spaces have been reclaimed by Red Hook's residents.

Now the area around the sprinklers has been spruced up with new play equipment, and Broughton often sees children running through the water spray in hot weather. According to Broughton, "We've still got a problem, but crime has declined. I think it's because of the court being here."

4

"I Didn't Go to Law School to Monitor Urines": Judges and Problem-Solving Courts[1]

Let me tell you about a colleague of mine on the bench.
He's actually the senior judge in our court,
who everybody would define as a traditional judge,
to the extent we all have a stereotype of that. Years ago,
he served as the judge in our local drug court.
Yesterday, he absolutely shocked me by saying
that his year on the drug court was the single most
meaningful experience he's had in twenty-two years
of being a judge. I said: "Gosh, that surprises me.
Why is that?" He said: "Because in many ways I was able,
with complete fidelity to all my principles,
to do a better job of being a judge in that context than
I ever was doing anything else.

—HON. TRUMAN MORRISON III,
District of Columbia Superior Court[2]

Problem-solving judges have raised concerns among both liberal and conservative commentators. On the right, problem solving conjures images of fuzzy-minded judges hell-bent on rehabilitation at the expense of accountability and individual responsibility. On the left, it raises the specter of a misguided judiciary unfettered by the restraints of the adversarial system, eager to send poor and defenseless defendants into lengthy social interventions for their own good, proportionality be damned.

There's no disguising the fact that the first generation of judges to preside over problem-solving courts was taking a real risk. Brooklyn judge John Leventhal's story is instructive. Leventhal's experience with problem-solving courts began back in the spring of 1996 in a conversation with administrative judge Michael Pesce. Pesce presented Leventhal with a fascinating opportunity, the chance to preside over a judicial experiment, the first of its kind in the state: a specialized domestic-violence court. Pesce was looking for a judge who was willing to explore new ways of handling cases, someone who was as good at forging partnerships as he was at parsing the law, and who didn't shy away from gut-wrenching decisions. The court would handle crimes that stood out not only for their violence, but also for the fact that the accused and their victims were intimately involved. The thinking behind the specialized court was simple: domestic violence cases demand a unique set of skills and knowledge from judges, attorneys, and social workers. Aggregating these cases in a single courtroom would make it easier to protect victims and to make more informed decisions about court orders.

Leventhal was intrigued. The idea of a domestic-violence court reminded him of why he went into the law in the first place. "A lot of judges and lawyers want to help people and the society at large," he later reflected, "but it's rare to get a case that actually means something to humanity. At the domestic-violence court, I feel like I'm doing meaningful work every day."[3]

Accepting Pesce's offer was hardly out of character for Leventhal, whose career is full of unexpected twists and turns. In the early 1970s, the Bronx native competed in Golden Gloves tournaments. When boxing didn't lead to fame and fortune, he started teaching math in a South Bronx middle school; and then, still searching for the right career, he decided that law was his calling. After fifteen years in private practice, Leventhal itched for something new. So he ran for judge—and won.

Leventhal hoped that Pesce had chosen him for the domestic-violence experiment because he was the best person for the job. But secretly he thought that Pesce was turning to him, a relative newcomer to the bench, because other more established jurists had turned him down. Handling domestic-violence cases did not exactly seem like a choice assignment. For one thing, Leventhal wasn't entirely sure he was up to the task. After all, what did he know about domestic violence? In private practice, he'd had only one domestic-violence case, and so far as a judge he'd handled just a single domestic-violence case.

While Leventhal felt he had much to learn, he knew enough to know that domestic-violence cases pose special challenges. These cases are hardly ever straightforward. Instead, they tend to be colored by the complex relationship between victim and accused. Unlike stranger-on-stranger crimes, in which victims almost always cooperate with authorities, victims of domestic violence are often reluctant witnesses. They try to drop charges, refuse to talk to prosecutors, and sometimes even testify on the defendant's behalf. Victims know their attackers intimately, often live with them for many years, and frequently have children in common. Many profess to be in love with their assailants. Even those who don't are often bound to defendants financially. The fact that victims have ongoing relationships with their batterers means that there is a very real risk of continued abuse. The bottom line is that domestic-violence cases are fraught with problems that go far beyond simply determining a defendant's culpability.

CHANGING PRACTICE

But the biggest challenge wasn't uncooperative victims; nor was it Leventhal's lack of knowledge about domestic violence. Leventhal knew that the hardest part of the job would be keeping victims safe. Defendants charged with domestic violence crimes routinely violated orders of protection—sometimes with tragic results.

In fact, when Leventhal was offered the job, the criminal justice system in New York City was still feeling the aftershocks from the murder of a local woman who had been killed by her boyfriend despite two orders of protection. In some quarters, blame for the widely reported murder fell on the shoulders of the judge who, three weeks earlier, had reduced bail for the offender. The presiding judge was vilified in the city's tabloids for months. Both the mayor and the governor called for his ouster.

Of course, the problems with the criminal justice system's response to domestic violence went beyond the failings of any individual courtroom. Nor was it exclusive to New York. Around the country, there was a growing concern—among feminists, victim advocates, scholars, and others—that the courts were not adequately equipped to protect victims or monitor compliance with orders of protection.

Historically, many police officers, judges, and prosecutors have viewed domestic-violence cases as a "private" or "family" matter.[4] Police, for example, often responded to reports of domestic violence by escorting the assailant around the block to "cool off," and then returning him home, where the abuse continued. If a case made its way to court, prosecutors frequently dropped the charges at the victim's request, and judges only sporadically issued orders of protection. Even when they did, the orders often proved ineffective—a 1996 study found that 60 percent were violated within one year. Another study found that more than one in six victims killed in domestic incidents had previously obtained orders of protection.[5]

In response to advocacy from the feminist movement and victim-rights groups, criminal justice leaders in the 1980s and 1990s began to respond with a variety of initiatives, including specialized domestic-violence units in police departments and prosecutors' offices, tougher criminal sanctions for abusers, and reforms that made protective orders easier to obtain. "There was a big push to increase arrests. States passed mandatory-arrest legislation and funded training for police," says law professor and domestic-violence expert Emily Sack.[6] Supporting these initiatives was the Violence Against Women Act, which Congress passed in 1994. The Act created a special office within the Department of Justice, which has provided funding and guidance to criminal justice agencies around the country as they try to respond more effectively to domestic violence.

From 1989 to 1998, domestic-violence filings in state courts increased 178 percent—a sign of both increased public awareness and more rigorous enforcement.[7] As more and more cases arrived in the nation's courts, the judiciary began to

adapt as well. Court systems, starting in the 1980s and picking up steam throughout the 1990s, began experimenting
with ways to improve their handling of domestic-violence
cases: some established separate calendars to hear only
domestic-violence cases; some began offering increased services to victims, such as links to shelters or financial assistance;
some focused on safety in the courthouse, providing separate
and secure waiting areas for victims and their children.

In some places, these efforts eventually evolved into full-
fledged domestic-violence courts. The first domestic-
violence court was launched in Quincy, Massachusetts, in
1987. Today, there are about 300 specialized domestic-
violence court initiatives around the country.[8]

"SOMETHING AWFUL MIGHT HAPPEN"

At the time Judge Pesce approached Leventhal in 1996, the
concept of a domestic-violence court was still fairly new.
There were only a handful of such courts around the country, but most shared two key goals: to improve victim safety
and to increase the accountability of offenders.[9]

In fact, "victim safety and offender accountability" is a
mantra repeated again and again by those who work in
domestic-violence courts. Since there is no scientific evidence that proves that perpetrators of domestic-violence can
be rehabilitated (and a fair amount of anecdotal evidence to
suggest the opposite), most domestic-violence courts scrupu-
lously avoid rehabilitation as an explicit goal. In a sense, this
sets domestic-violence courts apart from other problem-
solving courts. While drug courts and community courts
aspire to help offenders change their behavior, domestic-violence courts are almost single-mindedly focused on simply
ensuring that defendants abide by protective orders. If they

have any interest in treatment at all, it's focused on the victim, providing her with the services she needs to be protected from future harm.

The Brooklyn court was no exception. Victim safety took precedence. By handling all felony cases from the borough in a single courtroom, the court was designed to develop a focused expertise in domestic violence. Just as important, by assigning all cases to a single judge, the court sought to promote greater consistency. In the past, it was common for prosecutors who specialized in domestic violence to complain that "every judge had their own rules."[10]

In contrast, the new court would not simply issue an order of protection and then forget about it for months. Instead, the court would carefully monitor compliance with the order and swiftly sanction—with jail, if necessary—any violations. In addition, the court wouldn't adjourn cases for months at a time but instead would require defendants to return on a regular basis, if only to impress upon them that the court was closely watching them. Defendants would be required to participate in batterer intervention programs as a condition of bail. And there would be extra staff to work with victims and provide them with services, such as safe houses, financial aid, and job training.

In the end, Leventhal signed on to the experiment, even though he knew that despite rigorous court involvement, a tragedy might be unavoidable. "There's an emotional dynamic, and things can be unpredictable," Leventhal said. "I knew that I would always be worrying that something awful may happen."[11] Eight years after taking on the assignment, Leventhal's fear of tragedy hasn't waned: "What haunts me is the specter, the prospect that, God forbid, there's a fatality or a terrible beating. . . . I would think I am to blame."

"HIGH-RISK, LOW-BENEFIT, AND UNDESIRABLE"

Leventhal's hesitation about presiding over a problem-solving court was in many ways typical of his peers. "To many judges, assignment to a specialized domestic-violence docket is viewed as high-risk, low-benefit, and, consequently, undesirable," writes Susan Keilitz of the National Center for State Courts.[12] But it's not just domestic-violence courts that concern judges. Why are judges reluctant to preside over problem-solving courts? The reasons go much deeper than the apprehension of individual judges and reflect deep-seated institutional concerns about problem-solving courts and their implications.

Judges are trained to respect precedent and tradition, and, to many eyes, problem-solving courts represent the opposite: something new and unknown. As New York State chief judge Judith Kaye puts it:

> Lawyers, of course, are completely comfortable with the notion that the substantive law must change and adapt to meet changing social conditions. But they are distinctly less comfortable with the idea that the structures of the justice system may also need to evolve to meet current demands. I suppose this shouldn't be too surprising: my work uniform hasn't changed for centuries, and I do my job in a building smack out of ancient Athens. You don't need a degree in semiotics to conclude that ours is a profession that values formal stability and continuity.[13]

"Our branch of government tends to be the most tradition-bound branch of all," says Thomas Zlaket, chief justice of the Arizona Supreme Court. "We are the slowest to change, we're the most reluctant to change. It may have something to do with the fact that we are trained to rely on precedent. Our whole lives are precedent. The word precedent binds us."[14]

Tradition dictates that judges serve as neutral arbiters and that their work focus on process and penalties. But in a problem-solving court, judges are asked to focus on other issues as well, such as the underlying problems of defendants, the impact of criminal behavior on victims, and the implications of crime for a community. In short, in a problem-solving court, context matters in a way that it doesn't in most conventional courts.

Many judges are understandably concerned with expanding their scope of work in this way. Some wonder whether the problems that problem-solving courts address—such as drug addiction, mental illness, and domestic violence—are even solvable. Problem-solving judges are the first to admit that the challenges are sometimes insurmountable. Judge Raymond Norko, the founding judge of the Hartford Community Court, describes the challenges of addressing the problems of women engaged in prostitution: "They come in with so much baggage—drugs, mental-health problems, physical health complaints, along with economic structures—that make it very, very difficult to keep them out of the cycle [of crime]."[15] Similarly, the first drug-court judge in the country, the late Stanley Goldstein of Miami-Dade County, Florida, worried that "there was no way we were going to get people off crack cocaine. I saw people who had come out of the sewers so addicted to cocaine they would sell their firstborn."[16]

Beyond concerns about whether certain kinds of problems can even be solved, many judges also wonder about the appropriateness of problem-solving. Says Truman Morrison III of the District of Columbia Superior Court: "When you try and channel the energies of social change into the judicial branch, it's not a good fit. Judges' own personal worldviews shouldn't be unleashed under the guise of special courts."[17] Morrison's concerns are echoed by Denver district judge Morris B. Hoffman: "We are judges, not social workers or psychiatrists. We administer the criminal law because the criminal law is its own social end. It is not, or at least ought not to be, a means to other social ends."[18]

According to Richard Cappalli, a professor at Temple Law School,

> When judges move out of the box of the law and into working with individual defendants, transforming them from law-breaking citizens into law-abiding citizens, we have to worry. Because what has always protected the bench has been the law. Whenever a judge is approached by a disgruntled individual saying, "How could you do that?" The judge always says: "That wasn't me speaking—that was the law." If we take the mantle of the law's protections off of the judges and put them into these new roles, we have to worry about judicial neutrality, independence, and impartiality.[19]

Even judges engaged in problem-solving justice worry that by expanding their mandate, there's a chance they'll create new problems rather than solve existing ones. "I'm not sitting back and watching the parties and ruling," says Judge Cindy Lederman from Florida. "I'm making comments. I'm encouraging. I'm making judgment calls. I'm getting very involved with families. I'm making clinical decisions to some extent, with the advice of experts. So I have much greater opportunities, I think, to harm someone than I would if I just sat there, listened, and said guilty or not guilty."[20]

Judge Patricia Young, who presides over a community court in Boise, Idaho, also acknowledges that her work is "a lot messier" than conventional judging: "You're dealing with human issues and concerns in a more personalized way, trying to find out what's going on with these people so that the consequences we come up with are appropriate."[21]

SOFT ON CRIME?

Concerns about the complexity of cases and the chances of actually solving the problems of offenders only scratch the surface. In working to meet the new goals and imperatives of problem-solving courts, judges are raising important questions about the nature of judicial independence, the risks of paternalism, the efficacy of the adversarial system, and the tensions that exist between criminal justice imperatives (where public-safety concerns are paramount) and the dictates of social work (where the needs of the individual client are of primary concern).

The concern most often expressed about judges in problem-solving courts is that they've forsaken the rigors of law for the fuzzy world of psychology. Many judges in problem-solving courts have found themselves derided as "touchy-feely," "soft on crime," and "coddling." "The truth is that problem-solving courts always have to fight the knee-jerk reaction people have to throw everyone in jail," says Judge Norko of the Hartford Community Court, "Anything short of jail to a lot of people is not effective."[22]

But the truth of the matter is that problem-solving courts are competing against the rhetoric of jail more than the reality. Many offenders—particularly misdemeanor offenders and those convicted of nonviolent offenses—do not receive jail or prison sentences. Many others receive sentences of such short duration as to be almost meaningless as either deterrent or as incapacitation.

Problem-solving judges often make the case that their courtrooms are *tougher* than conventional courts. Indeed, in places like New York City, one of the underlying rationales for the first community court in Midtown was to strengthen sentences for low-level offenders. "The reality of it," says Judge Melanie May, a former drug-court judge, "is that anybody that goes through drug court does almost one hundred times more as far as treatment hours and attendance at court and toeing the line than most traditional probationers do who only have to go once a month to a probation officer." Judge Joseph Valentino, presiding judge of a drug court in Rochester, New York, puts it this way:

> I was really skeptical about drug courts at first, thinking that they were one of those liberal touchy-feely programs where you just pat somebody on the back, get them on probation and get them out of the courtroom. But after watching the drug treatment court in Rochester a couple of times, I realized that it was not a social worker type of court. It was the first time that I saw defendants having to take responsibility for their actions. Defendants were immediately accountable. The judge knew whether they were following their program within a couple of days, not months later.[23]

Judge Stephen V. Manley, who founded a drug court in Santa Clara, California, also rejects the notion that problem-solving courts are easy. He recounts a laundry list of complaints he has heard about problem-solving courts:

> "the judges are social workers; the judges don't hold people accountable; they're soft, fuzzy; they have no standards" . . . I think that's a great misconception. Problem-solving courts in my view are the most accountable courts we have, because

the judge is responsible for each and every individual. There's no passing the buck. They [defendants] are seen more often, followed more closely than any other defendants.[24]

TESTING THE LIMITS OF JUDICIAL AUTHORITY

Indeed, most problem-solving judges end up playing a vigorous role in the lives of offenders. Judging in a problem-solving court doesn't end when a disposition has been reached. Rather, problem-solving judges require offenders to return to court frequently to report on their progress in meeting the court's mandates. And over the course of many court appearances, judges in problem-solving courts often find themselves learning about offenders' home lives, children, and other personal issues that are normally well outside the concerns of a conventional judge.

According to Judge Jamey Weitzman, who presided over a drug court in Baltimore, the judge inquires "into many facets of offenders' lives, including employment, health and family life. In fact . . . the judge is familiar with each defendant in an almost parental role."[25] For drug-court advocates, these inquiries are justified by the idea that the court is trying not just to get the offender sober, but also to remove any other obstacles to a law-abiding life. Therefore, whether an offender has a stable home, a job, and a place to live are all the court's business. Yet such inquiries rub some observers the wrong way, raising the specter of judicial paternalism run amok at the expense of such important judicial values as neutrality and impartiality.

For the uninitiated, a judge's relationship with an offender in drug court can be almost shocking. New York judge Laura Ward's courtroom offers an example. Judge Ward is a no-nonsense personality. The daughter of a federal judge and herself a former prosecutor who worked on the team that put Gambino crime boss John Gotti behind bars, Ward is deeply respectful of the law and the power of tradition. Upon embarking on her career as a judge in the late 1990s, the last place she thought she'd end up was overseeing a drug court. "I didn't go to law school to monitor urines," Ward says.[26]

Ward now finds herself doing things that would have been anathema to her as a prosecutor. When an offender with nine months sobriety says she has family troubles, Ward asks for the details. The woman explains that her sixteen-year-old daughter was arrested in another county for stealing a car. Ward shakes her head, as if to say she understands the suffering teenagers impose on their parents. "I know she's putting you through a lot," Ward tells the mother, "but don't go back to drugs. It's not worth it."

Then Ward goes a step further. Rather than merely impart some encouraging words, Ward offers to help. "If you think it might help, I'd be happy to talk to your daughter," Ward says. The client smiles gratefully; she doesn't seem at all surprised by the offer. Ward makes clear her willingness to help by adding: "Maybe if it comes from a judge, it might have an impact."

Indeed, this notion—that judicial authority carries weight, that judges can make a difference—goes to the heart of the problem-solving enterprise. "I've found that we as judges have enormous psychological power over the people in front of us," says Rosalyn Richter, a former judge at the Midtown Community Court. "It's not even coercive power. It's really the power of an authority figure and a role model. You have power not only over that person, but over their family in the audience, over all the people sitting in that courtroom."[27]

Some fear that this power leads easily to an overly paternalistic judiciary. According to Steve Zeidman, a professor at the City University of New York law school, "[Problem-solving courts] are bringing [offenders] into the legal system and then in the course of providing much-needed help, we subject them to fair amounts of social control. . . . The danger of 'Big Brother' is very real."[28] John Stuart, the Minnesota state public defender, writes:

> The defense lawyer's job often is to ask people to look at both sides of the story. A public defender's perspective on "problem-solving courts," therefore requires two points of view: problem-solving courts can be just great. And they also can be very, very dangerous. Above all, they should not make the mistakes that have been made [in the past]. . . . Juvenile court, for example, was started in 1899 with the highest possible aspirations and ideals—and incorporated due process of law only in 1967.[29]

Colorado judge Morris B. Hoffman echoes Stuart's concern about problem-solving judges operating outside of due process: "I cannot imagine a more dangerous branch than an unrestrained judiciary full of amateur psychiatrists poised to 'do good' rather than to apply the law."[30] He describes drug-court judges as "a bizarre amalgam of untrained psychiatrists, parental figures, storytellers and confessors. . . . Judges have become, in the flash of an eye, intrusive, coercive and unqualified state psychiatrists and behavioral policemen, charged with curing all manner of social and quasi-social diseases, from truancy to domestic violence to drug use."[31]

Problem-solving judges offer two responses to these concerns. First, they argue that their problem-solving efforts occur at sentencing, after a case has been formally adjudicated

and a defendant has had an opportunity to exercise his constitutional rights. At the sentencing stage, a wide range of
inquiry—about extenuating circumstances and the impacts of
crime on individual victims and neighborhoods—is typically
permitted even in a conventional court. Problem-solving
judges argue that they are operating within this tradition. In
the process, they suggest that problem solving is not a departure from the judicial norm, but rather part of a rich tradition
of an engaged judiciary. For example, New York judge Juanita
Newton has argued that

> The process of judging, where judges use their authority to
> form an informed response to social problems, is simply not
> new, it is not unusual. It is what we do. Brown v. the Board
> of Education, for example, comes to . . . mind. And so, just
> as it is appropriate for judges to have informed responses to
> public macro issues, I think it is similarly appropriate for us
> to have those informed responses to micro personal issues,
> such as drug addiction for individuals, particularly when
> we know that it has [an] effect in the public milieu.[32]

IN THE COURTROOM

How do these issues—of paternalism, accountability, and the
limits of judicial authority—play themselves out in the courtroom? It's worth returning to where we started—with Judge
John Leventhal and the Brooklyn Domestic Violence Court.

Leventhal has presided over the court for eight years
now. He endeavors to communicate directly with each
defendant who comes before him. Rather than let an order
of protection speak for itself, or trust that a defense attorney will review the details of the order with his client, Leventhal looks every defendant in the eye and explains: "Mr.

Smith, this order of protection is my order of protection, not your wife's. If she invites you over to dinner, it will be the most expensive dinner you ever had because the next night you will be eating dinner in jail."

And because Leventhal retains a case from indictment through the completion of the sentence, he truly gets to know the defendants—and they get to know him. By frequently bringing defendants back to court for monitoring, Leventhal sends a message that he's closely following compliance.

Judge Leslie Leach, who for many years presided over a drug court in Queens, interacts not only individually with clients, but with the entire court audience. As he enters his wood-paneled courtroom, Leach shouts a general greeting. "Good morning, everyone," Leach says. "How are you doing?"

The offenders in the audience answer with a chorus of positive replies: "Good," "Fine," "OK."

Leach then asks a question, singling out a defendant in the audience: "Springtime, they tell me, is a tough time for recovery. Mr. Lloyd, why is springtime hard?"

"You're out more and can get into trouble," Lloyd replies.

Leach nods affirmatively. "That's right," he says, and then quotes a favorite twelve-step slogan: "Don't forget: people, places, and things."

Across town, in Judge Laura Ward's Manhattan courtroom, the approach is very much the same. Before every appearance, Ward holds a case conference with the court case manager, prosecutor, and defense attorney so that when the defendant appears before her, Ward knows exactly what's going on, including the results of urine tests, attendance history at the treatment program, and even the clinical observations of treatment staff.

"It says here that you're a follower and that you've started hanging out with the wrong crowd. That concerns me," says the judge, addressing a teenaged defendant as she looks over a treatment counselor's report. "Maybe you can find some other people to hang out with," says Ward, "people who won't lead you into trouble."

She then suggests that perhaps the teen should also strive to be a leader; rather than follow others, he should try to set a good example for his peers. The youth listens intently to the judge, nodding slowly. "I know you can do it," the judge says, encouragingly. "I'm keeping my fingers crossed that when you come back next month, I'll get a glowing report describing the progress you've made."

Ward draws from many sources in her conversations with defendants, including note cards on which she records personal data: this defendant has a baby, this one has an ailing parent, this one is applying to technical school. When she wants to be encouraging, these little facts work their way into her conversations with defendants. "How's the baby? Being a parent sure can be challenging." She calls one middle-aged man to the bench to show him his arrest photo. "See how awful you looked?" she said, holding up an image of despair—hair matted, swollen face, bewildered and hopeless. The man before Ward today is alert, hair combed, eyes far brighter. "You look great. You really do," the judge says. He nods knowingly as Ward encourages him to continue in treatment and maintain his sobriety.

To clients who are doing well, Ward offers boundless encouragement. But to those who have repeatedly failed, Ward is uncompromising. "I've given you two chances at treatment already. Why should I give you a third?" she asks one defendant. She makes a teenager spend the morning writing an essay explaining why he thinks she should be lenient after he left his residential treatment program without permission. In another case, before imposing a sentence of three to six years in prison, she unleashes an angry lecture about a defendant's repeated failure to comply with the court's treatment plan and his disrespectful attitude toward court staff.

Ward's manner is in some respects a performance, a form of theater that is not merely for the benefit of the individual client but for everyone in the courtroom. In fact, problem-solving judges frequently organize their calendars for maximum effect. Participants who are doing well in treatment are often the first called—not merely to reward them for their achievement, but to let the successful participants serve as an example for other defendants in the audience.

THE TEAM APPROACH

Whether a judge is an accomplished performer like Ward and Leach or more reticent, the bottom line is that a problem-solving judge is an active participant in court proceedings. Drug courts in particular extol the idea of the judge as the leader of the court "team," which includes defenders and prosecutors as well as social workers. "Because it's a team approach . . . you aren't fighting all the time with everybody," says Florida judge Melanie May, "We all work in the same direction."[33] Adds Judge Leach: "We'd like to think that the best interest of the defendant in treatment is the goal we all seek."[34]

The concept of "teamwork," and the idea that everyone in the courtroom, including the judge, is a "team player," is an important feature of many problem-solving courts. This idea makes some observers nervous. After all, if defenders and prosecutors are now part of the same team, what's left of adversarialism, a defining principle of our justice system?

"The obvious risk," writes Lisa Schreibersdorf, executive director of Brooklyn Defender Services, "is the erosion of zealous defense advocacy as the three participants—judge, prosecutor, and defense attorney—begin to consider themselves 'teammates.' "[35] Judge Jeff Tauber, former president of the National Association of Drug Court Professionals, says

> defenders need to look at this as a new approach that requires a level of teamwork and partnership that is not often seen. It requires defenders to take a step back, to not intervene actively between the judge and the participant, and allow that relationship to develop and do its work. . . . It really does demand that they partner and work very closely with both the court, treatment, and their former adversary, the prosecutor.[36]

Many defenders are uncomfortable with the expectation that they "take a step back." Mae Quinn, a public defender in the Bronx, argues that defense attorneys may feel pressure from judges, prosecutors, and other "team" members not to raise objections to the treatment mandate or the scope of a proposed sanction.[37]

Kathleen M. Cantella, a deputy public defender in Los Angeles County, strives to be a team player in drug court, and yet her cooperative spirit is tempered by vigilance. "I sit there quietly most of the time. I learned to cut the lawyer yap because the traditional public defender shtick isn't what these clients need," Cantella says. "But once in a while, I think I might hear something coming, and I have to jump up. . . . I have to ask my client to tell me what they're about to say, just to make sure they're not about to admit to some murder twenty years ago.' "[38]

While defenders' caution about problem solving is understandable, it is worth noting the lawyering that does take place in problem-solving courts. For example, in a drug court, up until a defendant opts to participate in treatment, the defense attorney is (or at least should be) engaged in advocating for the best possible deal for his client. In addition to contesting the merits of each case, defenders in drug courts also argue about eligibility criteria, the length of treatment sentences, and appropriate treatment modalities (for example, outpatient versus residential).

JUDICIAL INDEPENDENCE

In addition to keeping an eye on the quality of advocacy in the courtroom, a problem-solving judge has to remain equally vigilant to preserve judicial independence. The question for judges is: Does participation in a problem-solving court compromise a judge's ability to make independent decisions?

This question needs to be addressed if problem-solving courts are to operate within the code of judicial ethics—and if they are to persuade the judicial establishment, the bar, and the public that they are not tampering with fundamental legal principles. Judicial independence, after all, "ranks high in our nation's bundle of values," says Shirley Abrahamson, chief justice of Wisconsin's Supreme Court. Among other things, it enables judges "to resolve disputes free from threat of physical harm, financial interest, or popular or political pressure."[39]

Although we've been speaking of the team as a troika—involving only defense attorney, prosecutor, and judge—the team in many problem-solving courts also includes court-based case managers, treatment providers, probation officers, and others. A judge's job involves not only managing events inside the courtroom, but also managing the team: Have all relevant voices been consulted? Are team members providing timely and useful information? Are they being held accountable for their actions? And, when a conflict arises, does the judge have the distance and the clarity to resolve the dispute in a manner consistent with the law and the goals of the court?

"I wasn't trained in addiction or psychology," Judge Laura Ward of the Manhattan Treatment Court points out. "I need people who are experts in these areas to give me information." Ward, like many judges in problem-solving courts, believes that it's her job to weigh the information from the team, to consider all sides, and then to render judgment; in that way, she preserves her judicial distance and neutrality. "I always listen to what they have to say, although the final decision is always mine to make," she says.

Others aren't so sure. Jo-Ann Wallace of the National Legal Aid and Defender Association, worries about problem-solving courts relying too heavily on "expert" advice: "The danger lies in problem-solving courts' overstepping—basing sentencing decisions on the court's interpretations of social science research."[40]

Working within a "team" raises another important concern for judges—the danger of ex parte communication. Legal scholar Cait Clarke describes a disturbing field trip her criminal justice class took to a drug court: "We were brought behind the scenes . . . the players were at the table and the negotiating was going on about case resolution. My students turned to me and asked: Where's the defense lawyer? They weren't in the room." Clarke says the judge didn't think "he was having an ex parte experience . . . because the defendant had already pled guilty. . . . He felt that they were in the therapeutic stage. I think he thought that they were simply caring for a client."[41]

Clearly, judges, in relying on the advice of experts, need to be careful not to exclude defenders (or prosecutors, for that matter) from the discussion. "What concerns me is that a problem-solving court would decide that the most effective way to deliver treatment is by having the professionals decide it without littering up the room with obstructionist lawyers," says Judge Truman Morrison III. Judge Judy Harris Kluger, who oversees problem-solving courts across New York State, agrees that "there should never be a discussion about a case and a defendant without the prosecutor and the defense counsel being present."[42]

Some also question whether judges, by working in a court with a narrow focus—such as domestic violence or drug treatment—will eventually succumb to the undue influence of advocates with whom they come into regular contact. Writing about domestic-violence courts, Susan Keilitz of the National Center for State Courts notes that "specialized judges can lose their neutrality, or the appearance of neutrality, by becoming more educated to the effects of domestic violence and collaborating with the advocacy community."[43]

But critics have not made a convincing case that problem-solving judges are somehow different from conventional judges with regard to outside expertise. No one would ever accuse a judge of being too much of an expert on complex commercial litigation or the Uniform Commercial Code— why would they make that argument for domestic-violence cases or cases involving addicted offenders? Moreover, judges are routinely asked to make subtle decisions regarding whether or not to exclude evidence—why can't they bring the same kind of nuance to contextual information about the nature of domestic violence or the history of crime in a specific neighborhood? Shouldn't we provide judges with as much information as possible?

Judges in problem-solving courts say they receive far more information on which to base a decision than would otherwise be available in a conventional court. At each court appearance, a problem-solving judge is provided with a detailed report: Has the defendant been attending AA meetings? Has the defendant abided by orders of protection? Has the defendant stayed clean? What potential obstacles, if any, threaten the defendant's future compliance with court orders? With this information, judges can use their authority to prevent little slips from turning into major violations, and can react swiftly and sternly to situations that might threaten public safety.

Theoretically, judges in conventional courtrooms should have access to similar information—from pretrial agencies, probation departments, and lawyers—to make sure all the facts, all the mitigating circumstances, all the issues that really matter, are weighed before a decision is made. The reality is that few of them get information as detailed, accurate, and up-to-date as problem-solving judges do.

To understand how a problem-solving court helps judges access information, consider the experience of Judge Leslie Leach. Before Leach took charge of the Queens Treatment Court in 1998, he sent a number of offenders into treatment on his own. Unfortunately, he says, he didn't have a complete understanding of addiction and the process of recovery; he also didn't know very much about the programs to which he was referring offenders. "When I did the cases on my own, I'd say, 'How is she doing? Is she OK?,' but I didn't know about the details of treatment—what orientation was, what it was like working in the kitchen, doing door duty, what a contract was."[44]

To do an effective job, Leach needed more information, the kind of information that is routinely available through the apparatus of the problem-solving court. As judge of the Queens Treatment Court, he received detailed reports on

the progress of each offender. He met regularly with representatives of treatment agencies and visits their facilities.
And he had access to the latest research and best practices
in the field of substance-abuse treatment thanks to the
court's specialized staff.

"Now that I know what all those things are, it allows me
to be more effective. I'm talking directly to the defendant, and
I can forewarn them that a contract is difficult, and I can give
them advice for getting through it," Leach says. "The drug
court has given me greater insight into where the client
stands, what his needs are and how to proceed effectively."[45]

Judge Jo Ann Ferdinand, who has presided over the
Brooklyn Treatment Court since its inception in 1996, tells a
similar story. "Problem-solving courts allow judges to develop a substantive expertise in a particular area," she notes.
"When I was in criminal court, I used to give defendants one
chance at drug treatment, and if they messed up, I would
give them a harsher sentence or disposition. But since presiding at the Brooklyn Treatment Court, I've learned that
recovery is not an event; it's a process. It's not all or nothing.
Giving them just one shot at rehabilitation is not helpful. At
the Treatment Court, I follow defendants' progress in treatment and try to maximize their chances for success."[46]

Ultimately, the impact of problem-solving courts on judicial independence may come down to the personality of
individual judges, just as it does in conventional courts. As
anyone who has practiced in criminal court knows, some
judges rely heavily on the advice of experts, and others do
not. Some judges are known as soft touches, others are notorious for being hanging judges. The point is that while our
courts are designed to promote the rule of law, judicial tem-
perament always has an impact on how a case is decided.
Although we have long strived for a court system devoid of

bias and inconsistency, the reality is that any system designed and implemented by humans will always be idiosyncratic. The relevant question is not "Do problem-solving courts have the potential for a negative impact on core judicial values like judicial independence?" but rather "Are they any more likely to undermine these values than conventional courts?" The answer seems to be no.

WORKING WITH COMMUNITIES

Another concern raised about problem-solving judges involves their active engagement with the local community. They speak before community groups; they participate in advisory boards designed to air community concerns; some may even advocate for new community resources or programs. Problem-solving judges reach out to the community in an effort to achieve a number of goals: to better understand the context in which crime occurs so they can fashion better dispositions; to build more effective partnerships between the court and social-service providers; and, ultimately, to improve public trust and confidence in justice.

This orientation challenges the traditional picture of a judge as someone isolated from worldly events. Isolation has, in fact, become synonymous with judicial purity and objectivity. A judge in isolation is "above the fray" and thus inoculated from charges of bias or undue influence. This caution among judges has translated into a code of conduct that expects judges to be circumspect in all their dealings with the community.

It's worth noting, however, that this culture of isolation is not required by the Judicial Code of Conduct but is socially prescribed. The Judicial Code of Conduct does bar judges from commenting on a pending or impending case, but it "does not prohibit judges from making public statements in the court of their official duties or from explaining for public information the procedures of the court." The code also notes that "[a] judge may speak, write, lecture, teach and participate in other extra-judicial activities concerning the law, the legal system, the administration of justice and non-legal subjects. . . . As a judicial officer and person specially learned in the law, a judge is in a unique position to contribute to the improvement of the law, the legal system and the administration of justice."[47]

Judges in problem-solving courts recognize that isolation has a price. One consequence of isolation is that many judges have only the dimmest understanding of the impacts their actions have on the community. For the community, the price is often a loss of faith in the workings of the court. "The reason there is diminishing confidence in judges generally is because judges have isolated themselves from the communities we serve," says Judge Veronica Simmons McBeth, presiding judge of the Los Angeles Municipal Court. "We don't go out into the community and listen to what their concerns are."[48]

For judges in problem-solving courts, understanding community concerns is an essential component of their work on the bench. A community court, for example, depends on input from citizens in order to respond to community problems and develop effective solutions. While many judges might question the value of engaging the community, judges in problem-solving courts say the insight they gather by meeting regularly with the community has proven to be invaluable. In fact, both courts and communities can realize gains. Communities can educate judges about the realities of life in their neighborhoods, while judges have an opportunity to explain how the judiciary really works.

Judge McBeth offers this example. As she explains, a citizen of Los Angeles wrote her a letter that said, in effect: "Dear Judge McBeth, I have heard an awful lot about you, and, boy, it was all bad." The letter-writer went on to describe problems in the community, such as rampant prostitution and drug dealing. McBeth called the writer, who invited McBeth to attend a civic association meeting. Curious about what she would hear, McBeth decided to attend.

> When I went there, two important things happened. One, I had a chance to find out why they were mad at me. They thought the role of the supervising judge meant I could tell all fifty-two judges who sit in criminal court in the City of Los Angeles how to sentence, right? . . . Once I explained to them how important it is that judges are independent when they make their individual sentences, they all agreed and thought it was good. . . . But the most important thing that happened at that meeting was I stayed and listened to all the problems that they were having.[49]

The Midtown Community Court in New York offers another example of judicial-community interaction. The Midtown Court brings the judge, court staff, and community members together for monthly meetings to discuss neighborhood conditions. Community residents let the court know about hot spots where crime is concentrated, and the court works with community members and other agencies to address the problem. Among other things, the court has helped organize community clean-ups, worked with local property owners to improve street lighting to discourage crime, and deployed teams of social workers to link homeless people to services before they get into trouble.

Aware that some observers would worry that the court was

violating the separation-of-powers doctrine and treading upon the territory of the legislative and executive branches, judges at the Midtown Community Court did not dive thoughtlessly into working with the community but rather took a cautious approach. "In the early days of the Midtown Community Court, there were many judges—and I must say that I was one of them—who worried that by meeting with the community we would be opening the court up to criticism," says Judge Judy Kluger, the Court's first presiding judge:

> It was something I was very concerned about initially. But I realized that we are public officials and there is nothing improper or incorrect with us speaking to members of the public. I had been afraid that people would talk about particular cases and would try to influence me in some way, but I realized after the first advisory board meeting that I attended that they just wanted to express their appreciation for the court and have an interaction with the judge. The meetings created a spirit of partnership and collaboration that allowed community members to embrace ideas such as having defendants perform community service in their neighborhoods. They even volunteered ideas for where to send defendants and what they should do. The meetings resolved any distrust between the court and the community and were beneficial in helping the court grow.[50]

It is not only judges in community courts who have come to think of themselves as brokers and conveners. Judges in a range of problem-solving courts have made working with people and organizations outside the courthouse a basic part of their work. Judge Leventhal in the Brooklyn Domestic Violence Court, for example, hosts monthly meetings that bring together prosecutors, defenders, victim advocates, batterer-intervention programs, service providers, religious leaders, and community activists. At one meeting, Leventhal learned from corrections-department officials that they almost never knew when an order of protection was in effect. That meant that prisoners could, with impunity, write or call their victims from jail. In response, Leventhal and the domestic-violence court developed a protocol for keeping jails informed about the orders of protection that pertain to their prisoners—and encouraged jails to punish any violations.

WHY DO IT?

No examination of judges in problem-solving courts can be complete without asking a fundamental question: Why have so many judges around the country decided to create or participate in these novel courts? The short answer is dissatisfaction—with their jobs, with the tools at their disposal, and with the "revolving door" that returns the same offenders to their courtrooms again and again.

One of the biggest frustrations for criminal-court judges is the sense that their decisions don't really matter, that despite sentences of probation and jail, offenders eventually get arrested again and communities never become appreciably safer. Almost any state court judge can relate to the experience of Judge Legrome Davis, who oversees criminal courts in Philadelphia. "In the course of one year, I had five thousand felony defendants plead in front of me and get sentenced," Davis says. "I spent the next five years of my life watching them come back to court with an array of problems."[51]

Judge Ward tells a similar story: "Sitting in arraignments, I quickly realized that jail wasn't the answer. You'd put them in jail on Monday for a crack pipe, only to have them back in court on Wednesday for something new." On the other side of the country, Judge Stephen Manley of the Santa Clara drug court echoes the very same sentiments. "I've spent most of my career as a judge working with criminal cases," Manley says.

> When you begin sentencing the children of those you sentenced . . . you have to ask yourself, Have you made any change? Have you brought about anything you intended to by your sentencing previously? When you see that [what you're doing] is not having any desired effect in reducing recidivism, or changing people's lives, or effectively protecting victims, or having accountability, then you begin to question why we're doing the same thing over and over again.[52]

What Manley is describing is a conversion narrative experienced by many problem-solving judges—the moment the light bulb went off and they realized that the way they had been taught to handle cases was not having the desired effect. Almost invariably, this is what drives judges to try a problem-solving approach. Many who have taken this step do so over the objections of their colleagues on the bench. And many do so despite having their own reservations about the potential implications for their professional identity and the integrity of courts as an institution. Judge Leslie Leach of New York, for instance, still wonders if he's helped or hurt his career by presiding over a drug-treatment court: "I still sometimes wonder if serving in a drug court is a plus or minus. Should I be doing more trials? Should I be handling more high-profile cases?"[53]

The courage that it took for the first generation of problem-solving judges to make this step should not be underestimated.

FROM THE MARGINS TO THE MAINSTREAM

One of the challenges that confronts the problem-solving movement is how to reach beyond the first wave of problem-solving judges to engage the rest of the judiciary, many of whom will be quite resistant to the idea of tinkering with their traditional role. But there are some hints that state court judges may be more open to the idea of problem-solving than it might appear at first glance. A fall 2001 poll conducted by researchers at the University of Maryland surveyed more than 500 state court judges about problem-solving courts and the issues they address. A surprisingly large percentage of judges—whether they knew about problem-solving courts or not—were eager to assume a larger role in addressing the plight of victims, the public safety concerns of communities, and the underlying problems of defendants. For example, over 80 percent of the judges surveyed said judges should be involved in helping to reduce drug abuse among defendants. A similar percentage agreed that judges should play a role in protecting domestic-violence victims from continued violence and helping get mentally ill defendants into treatment.

Ninety percent of the judges surveyed reported that they wanted to be involved in ensuring that substance-abusing defendants attend court-ordered treatment and that defendants in domestic-violence cases attend batterer-intervention programs. And over 60 percent of the judges said they should work with community groups on neighborhood safety and quality-of-life concerns.

The survey offers a snapshot of an engaged judiciary increasingly willing to roll up its sleeves and get involved in addressing the kinds of problems they see on a daily basis. This willingness to take on new responsibilities is particularly

noteworthy because it represents a fairly dramatic departure from the conventional thinking about judicial attitudes. As recently as 1989, judges generally favored a hands-
off approach to problems like drug addiction and domestic
violence. Temple University researcher John Goldkamp
recalls attending a meeting that year at which "high-rank-
ing court officials in the nine most populous jurisdictions
spoke about court strategies that would process drug cases
more quickly." He says the officials "coolly ignored sugges-
tions to develop court-based treatment approaches." When
one judge argued "that the answer was not to be found in
making the machinery of justice spin faster, but rather in
developing an effective strategy of court-supervised drug
treatment in a way that had never before been attempted in
the criminal courts," the reaction from fellow judges was
"embarrassed silence and out-of-hand dismissal of ideas
that were viewed as being behind the times."[54]

Today, the response would be very different. In 2000, all
fifty state court chief judges (together with all fifty state
court administrators) unanimously passed a resolution
endorsing problem-solving justice. The American Bar Association quickly followed suit. One reason for this sea change
in attitudes is the research that has been published to date
about the results that problem-solving courts have
achieved. While there is certainly a need for additional
study, the early findings suggest that problem-solving
courts are making strides toward achieving their goals. This
includes community-court research that reports reduced
local crime and disorder; drug-court studies that document
reduced drug use and recidivism among drug-court participants; and domestic-violence-court research that tracks
significant reductions in probation violations and dismissal
rates for domestic-violence offenders (see chapter 6).[55]

"Judges see a lot of failure and not many successes, but since I've been at the drug court, I've seen quite a few successes, and that spurs me on," says Judge Joseph Valentino of Rochester, New York.[56]

Just as important as the results have been the high job-satisfaction levels reported by the first generation of problem-solving judges. For Judge Sharon Chatman, a California drug-court judge, it boils down to this: "You really have a chance to make a big difference in the lives of people."[57]

5

Success Stories

The Court saved me.

—KIM, former prostitute

The judges and attorneys who staff problem-solving courts are willing to experiment with new practices and procedures for one reason: because they think it will help them change the lives of victims, defendants, and neighborhood residents. This chapter tells the stories of four individuals whose lives were changed for the better by a community court, drug court, and domestic-violence court.

KIM

Kim first started prostituting at the age of twenty.[1]

Although she spent the next seventeen years selling her body on the streets of New York, Kim seems an unlikely candidate for the school of hard knocks. A voracious reader, she was raised by a churchgoing grandmother in a close-knit family in Harlem. She delights in describing a precocious childhood. She could write her name by the age of three. Her relatives often told her she was the smartest child in the family. She emphasizes that she was a well-loved child. Proud of her academic ability, Kim spent three years in college as an accounting major.

But the summer after her junior year, Kim was having trouble finding a summer job. On a dare, she took a weekend job as a stripper. It was her first step down a path that would lead her to life on the streets.

A tall, slender African-American woman, Kim, now forty, retains the statuesque bearing that once led her to contemplate a modeling career. She dresses with flair and walks with a confident stride. Kim's features are still pretty, but her face reflects the wear of living through hard times.

Despite Kim's happy childhood memories, the seeds of her later misfortune were sown while she was still young. At the age of thirteen, she was lured to an apartment by an acquaintance and raped by him and his friends. Kim thinks this event explains some of her willingness to sell her body later on. "I've tried to psychoanalyze it, and I must have lost some sense of self-respect and love for my body to be able to prostitute," she says.

Gesturing toward her heart, Kim attributes her ability to leave prostitution to the inner sense of right and wrong she retained from her early upbringing. When she speaks of her teenaged son, who is currently having trouble with school, her eyes fill with regret. "I wasn't there for him," she says of his childhood years that she missed while living the life of a hooker.

But when she started, regrets were the furthest things from Kim's mind. Kim ended up working at the strip joint the rest of the summer. At first, she says, she still planned to return to college in the fall. But that summer she fell in love with a man who introduced her to cocaine. Kim never went back to school.

For years, Kim's life consisted of going to work at night, getting high, and shopping for skimpy outfits to wear on the strip stage. "I envisioned myself as this night queen. I got to really think I was the superstar of the night world," Kim says today, marveling at her self-delusion.

When the strip joint closed, Kim thought about going back home and returning to college. But she was too far gone. Crack had become the focus of her life. She still remembers her first night of prostitution vividly—especially the money she made: $100 for the first half-hour; $700 by the end of the evening. "I'd never had that kind of money—hundreds of dollars in my hand instantaneously. It was a thrill," she says.

In 1987, Kim gave birth to a son, who lived with her grandmother while Kim went back to prostitution. Guilt over abandoning her son "made me want to be high all the time," she remembers. A baby daughter, born in 1991, was taken from her custody by the city's child-protection agency. She slipped further into depression and drugs.

Under pressure from her family, Kim made several attempts to get off drugs, but she always went back to smoking crack. For years, Kim's home was a room in a dilapidated Midtown motel that she had fixed up with red velvet drapes to receive her regular customers. When she wasn't there, she was on the street or, with increasing frequency, in the criminal justice system.

Kim's arrests for prostitution—eighteen between 1994 and 1999—brought her into contact with the Midtown Community Court. Today, Kim could not be clearer: "The court saved me," she says.

But it would be a long, halting process. At the start, Kim seemed an unlikely prospect for salvation from the streets.

She consistently failed to show up for the community-service assignments mandated by the judge. Those failures landed her in jail more than once. She ran away from several residential drug-treatment programs that the court had ordered her to attend. After jumping ship, she would be picked up by police on a warrant and brought back to the court, where she inevitably faced harsher sentencing.

Time after time, Kim arrived at the courthouse for court-mandated drug counseling in a drug-induced stupor, almost falling out of her chair in the waiting room, one clinical staff worker there remembers. But Kim remembers mainly the kindness and personal attention she received—a stark contrast to the regular criminal court. Midtown's social workers and counselors "reach out and touch people," Kim says. "You actually feel like you know them. It is so much different than the courts downtown. The courts downtown are cold: you're just arrested. In community court, the staff were my friends, and they were trying to help me."

The court's clinical director at the time, social worker John Megaw, saw Kim for individual counseling sessions on several occasions over the five-year period she had contact with the court. He remembers Kim becoming increasingly unkempt as the drugs took hold. "She was clearly very articulate and had an educational base," Megaw recounts. "She had made this sharp detour into drugs and partying. Once she was in that life, it was hard to put the brakes on."

In their counseling sessions, Megaw spoke directly to the academic ambitions Kim still harbored. As Kim remembers it, "He would look at me and say, 'You're so much better than this. Do you want to finish college? You can do it, Kim.' He'd say, 'You're not going to be pretty forever. You've got your son to think about. What will happen to him when he's a teenager if you're not there?'"

Megaw describes his strategy as a tenacious campaign to persuade Kim to focus on the positive things in her life outside the world of prostitution and drugs. "I could tell from the gleam in her eye when we talked about her education that it was a genuine concern. And she was very connected with her grandmother. There were these flags you could raise that could get her to connect in a positive way. She had enough of a superego that she knew prostitution was wrong and she didn't want to continue it. You needed to remind her by hitting the buttons on the positive things in her life—her education, her grandmother, and her son."

As the years passed, with each new arrest Kim came to dread most of all not the prospect of incarceration but the disappointment on her counselors' faces—and the sorrowful question, "You're still here?"

The court's message to Kim became a constant drumbeat, delivered in the courtroom, during counseling, and even on the street. Outreach workers from the court walked the streets of Midtown at night, offering to help prostitutes get out of the business. Recalling her encounters with the outreach workers, Kim says today that they were "crucial" in getting her to understand the urgency of making the transition out of "the life."

The words of one outreach worker made a particularly vivid impression on her: "He said, 'Kim, you know you're eventually going to go back to the mainstream of life. You're just too smart of a girl. So why waste another minute of your precious time out here on the street?' And he was so right."

After Kim had frittered away several opportunities to avoid jail by performing community restitution and attending drug treatment, the other shoe finally dropped—she was sentenced to sixty days in jail in 1997. Even this wake-up call was not enough. Kim was arrested again in January 1999.

Eileen Koretz, the presiding judge at the Midtown Community Court, gave Kim a choice: six months behind bars or ten
days on the work crew cleaning the courthouse building.
Kim chose the community service, and for a change, she
actually completed the sentence as ordered.

After years of working prostitution at night and sleeping
during the day, the obligation to get up in the morning for
community service put her back in a daytime routine—and
made it increasingly difficult to ply her trade at night.
"After a while, I actually started to feel like I had a job. It
made me want to have a real job," Kim says. "It gave me a
sense of accomplishing something."

Kim began taking some concrete steps in the right direction. She moved in with her grandmother. She started
attending Narcotics Anonymous. She returned to the
church. And she made a commitment to stay sober.

But when it came time to hunt for a job, she was surprised to discover that despite her education, "Nobody
would give me a chance." Seventeen years of prostitution
had left a big hole in her résumé.

Eager for employment, Kim signed up in May 2000 for the
Midtown Community Court's on-site job-training program,
which gives participants work experience they can put on
their résumé. On her first day, "She had a white shirt on and
she looked so fresh and ready, eager to go," remembers John
Megaw. "She had stepped out of this darkness, turning her
back on drug use and prostitution. We all felt, 'Here's the
woman we thought we would see, right in front of us.' "

Kim's claims of academic talent turned out to be more
than empty boasts, according to Jeff Hobbs, director of
recruitment for the training program. "I thought it was the
drugs talking. But she backed it up," says Hobbs. "She was a
stellar student. She was very verbal. She had leadership

qualities. If there was a group presentation, she led it."

Kim was even asked to write an article about the program for a neighborhood newspaper. She wrote: "This amazing 10-week program gave me the help I desperately needed. . . . They offered me up-to-date office-services training such as valuable basic computer skills, mailroom operations, typing, faxing, copying, shipping and receiving. I also learned the soft skills of business, like dressing for success, having a winning attitude and the fine art of communication. I was sent out on interviews. I am ecstatic to say, I not only got a job, I am still working."[2]

Kim is now a taxpayer and has ambitions to go into advertising, where she hopes to apply her flair for writing. As for the community court, Kim makes her debt clear: "If it were not for them, I might still be out there."

PATRONIA RUSSELL

Forty-two-year-old Patronia Russell first came to the Red Hook Community Justice Center as a tenant on the verge of being evicted from her apartment, along with her four children.

New York City's public housing authority had brought Russell to court for failure to pay her rent. Russell's saga had begun years before, when her husband left her and took up with another woman. Chaos ensued. The household income took a nosedive. Russell's nine-year-old daughter began having social and academic problems at school. To top it all off, "I was drinking like a champ," admits Russell.

Turning to booze was not typical behavior for Russell, who is a stocky woman who expresses her opinions forcefully. She is not afraid to tell drug dealers to get off her stoop. She proudly details the accomplishments of the tenant patrol she helped organize, and laughs at her inability to say no to the many requests for her barbeque at community picnics.

But in her distraught state, Russell admits, she stopped paying the rent. When dunning letters started arriving, she ignored them, hoping that the problem would go away by itself. By the time she realized this strategy wasn't working, she was shocked by the sum she owed—more than $5,000. It was not a sum that Russell, who was surviving on welfare and social security insurance, could afford to pay.

For almost a year and a half, Russell traveled back and forth to the housing court in downtown Brooklyn and to the local welfare office, trying without success to negotiate with the city's massive bureaucracy. In the fall of 2002, Russell received a final notice informing her that a marshal would be arriving within a few days to evict her. The eviction notice, says Russell, "gave me a scare. I was on a banana peel." She was especially worried because her eldest daughter was due to deliver a baby any day. She envisioned herself, her children, and all of their possessions out on the street.

But in some ways, the timing was fortunate. Unbeknownst to Russell, instead of going downtown, her case would be heard at the Red Hook Community Justice Center. Russell was close to tears when she first appeared before Judge Alex Calabrese. "They want to take my keys, judge," she told him. At the court hearing, Russell, who could not afford an attorney, asked the judge to give her time to get the money together. But the housing agency's lawyer told the court he wanted Russell evicted immediately.

Before rendering a decision, Calabrese referred Russell's case to the Justice Center's on-site housing resource center, which works to resolve landlord-tenant disputes through mediation. Housing specialist Alice Tapia was assigned to the case. After meeting with Russell and making a few phone calls, Tapia discovered that a large portion of Russell's back rent should have been paid by the welfare agency directly to the housing authority. Unfortunately, this bureaucratic transfer of funds between city agencies never happened.

Informed that Russell was on the verge of eviction, the welfare agency agreed to pay $4,800 in back rent. Armed with this information, Tapia told the judge that the chances of a negotiated agreement between Russell and the housing authority were good. At that point, Judge Calabrese issued an order staving off the eviction: "Where there is a light at the end of the tunnel, I'll give people a chance," he says. "No one likes to see families evicted, especially when the family is caught between two city agencies."

In the end, everyone left the negotiating table a winner. Russell agreed to contribute two months of back rent, which meant the housing authority would receive nearly all that it was owed. By agreeing to the mediated settlement, the housing authority also avoided the court costs it would have borne as part of a contested eviction proceeding. In return, the agency forgave Russell part of her back rent and agreed to adjust her rent downward to reflect her reduced income. The housing authority also agreed to fix Russell's broken intercom and door.

But that wasn't the end of Russell's story. Over the course of her involvement with the Justice Center, she had learned of the court's AmeriCorps community-service program, which offers participants a living stipend and job training in return for a year's worth of service to the community. Russell signed up for the program. Her first assignment was to help out in a public-housing management office, where she received high marks for her work.

Had it not been for the involvement of the Red Hook Community Justice Center, Russell believes she would probably have been evicted. "I didn't have nobody at that courthouse [downtown] to help me out," she says. In the days that followed, Russell had ample opportunity to remember Judge Calabrese's words in court: "He said, 'Don't put her out. Give her a chance.' He knew I was trying, so he helped me out a whole lot."

DAMON FUSEYAMORE

Russell's interaction with the court system was, to put it mildly, an unusual one. An eviction case involving a low-income tenant that ends not with heartache but with back rent paid, repairs made, and the tenant on the path to gainful employment? It simply doesn't happen in conventional courts.

In many respects, the story of Damon Fuseyamore is even more remarkable. By 1997, getting arrested for drug possession was nothing new for Damon Fuseyamore; after all, it had happened four times before. But when he got arrested in May 1997, something was different. This time he was charged with a drug sale as well as possession. Given his record and the seriousness of the charges, he was facing up to twenty-five years in prison.

Fuseyamore knew his life hung in the balance, so he didn't think twice when he was offered the chance to plead guilty and enter drug treatment instead of prison. If he completed treatment successfully, the charges against him would be dismissed and the case would be wiped off his criminal record. If not, he would have to do his time in prison.

Five years after seizing this unexpected opportunity and entering the Brooklyn Treatment Court, Fuseyamore is forty years old, drug-free, and employed. But as he tells it, the odds against him were substantial.

By 1997, Fuseyamore had been smoking crack for over a decade. Because of his addiction, he had lost his job as an auto mechanic. In 1990, he failed out of a residential treatment program that his parents had asked him to enter. The next seven years were spent on the streets as a crack addict. When he arrived at the Brooklyn courthouse, he looked like a toothpick, his 5-foot-8-inch frame carrying only 129 pounds.

"He looked awful and skinny, because crack addicts don't eat," remembers Judge Jo Ann Ferdinand of Brooklyn Treatment Court. "His family had pretty much had it. They were in court with him and said all they wanted was for him to get some help."

Fuseyamore may have been desperate to avoid prison, but that doesn't mean that he was immediately able to walk the straight and narrow. After Ferdinand gave him the chance to attend treatment, his next move was to run away. "My addiction had the best of me," he admits. He went back to living on the street, sleeping in a janitor's closet, and scoring to feed his habit. But he couldn't forget the judge's warning that she would send out a warrant for his arrest and send him to prison if he skipped out of treatment.

Fearing the consequences, he returned voluntarily to court just before the judge was about to issue a warrant for his arrest. In addition to his fear of jail, Fuseyamore had another motivation. His girlfriend was about to give birth to his son. "I didn't want my son to see me as an addict," he says.

Because Fuseyamore had taken the initiative to return to court, Judge Ferdinand let him back into treatment. She acknowledges that her approach is at odds with most conventional judges. "Had he pled guilty in a conventional court with a promise of probation and then gotten into trouble, the likelihood is he would have been sentenced to state prison for as much as four to seven years," Ferdinand says. In truth, in a conventional court, it would have been unlikely that Fuseyamore would have even gotten treatment in the first place.

Ferdinand stresses that she typically gives defendants "numerous chances," not because she is a soft touch but because she has learned from addiction experts that relapse is often a normal part of the recovery process. But before Ferdinand gave Fuseyamore a second bite at the apple, she gave him a sanction—as is her standard policy. She increased the mandated time in treatment and declared a zero-tolerance policy if he left the program. "I told him if he split again, there would be serious consequences," recalls Ferdinand.

Despite Ferdinand's warning, there would be more bumps along the road for Fuseyamore. "I had an attitude like 'Change me if you can,'" he recalls. At one point, the residential program removed all of his privileges as a penalty for having sex with another client—a violation of the program's rules. In response, Judge Ferdinand extended his time in treatment again, further delaying the dismissal of his case.

For all his setbacks, Fuseyamore never once produced a "dirty urine," testing positive for drugs. So what persuaded him finally to get clean? He says it was a combination of factors. First and foremost was his relationship with the judge. "I was kind of scared of her," he remembers. "This was my second chance, and I didn't think I'd have a third chance."

As time went on, he started looking forward to his regular court appearances and conversations with the judge, whose demeanor gradually changed from severe to encouraging as she praised him for his progress. "Those things make you feel good," he says, adding that the court gave him a sense of purpose.

The court also put Fuseyamore back on the road to supporting himself financially—an integral component of the drug-court mandate. While in the program, Fuseyamore took a brushup course in auto mechanics. A vocational counselor sent him for an interview to a bus company, where he got a job as a mechanic's helper. With each success, he says, "I started getting respect for myself," which in turn helped keep him sober.

The weight that Fuseyamore gives to the judge's role in his recovery is echoed by other drug-court participants. Research suggests that offenders thrive on praise from the judge, and dread disappointing the judge by poor performance.[3] Even after graduating from the treatment court, Fuseyamore's relationship with the judge continues to be important to him. He keeps in touch with the court on an informal basis, returning to speak to program participants and to converse with the judge. "I go there to say, 'Thank you.' That's the type of relationship I have with the court here," he reports proudly.

When Fuseyamore visits, Ferdinand makes a fuss over him and invites him to sit in a place of honor next to the court officers and attorneys. "This is a guy who's got a good job, who's doing the right thing for his family, who has turned his life around," she says.

Today, Fuseyamore barely resembles the skinny, strung-out addict who first showed up in Ferdinand's court. Weighing in at 200 pounds, he jokes that he could probably afford to lose some weight. He works two jobs as an auto mechanic to make ends meet. He makes it clear that he puts raising his son first in his life. If he hadn't had the court hammer hanging over his head, he believes he never would have recovered from his addiction. "I would probably have gotten killed using drugs," he says. "The court makes you stay in treatment."

PAMELA ISAAC

Using coercive authority in new ways is one of the hallmarks of problem-solving courts. Usually, this means providing offenders with the structure and support they need to avoid returning to court again and again. But there are many cases where this approach doesn't make sense, where offenders need, instead, to understand that criminal behavior, particularly violent criminal behavior, has real consequences. This message is important not just for offenders but for victims as well.

From her appearance, it's easy to tell that Pamela Isaac loves beautiful and unusual things. Preparing to teach an after-school arts-and-crafts class in the basement of a Greenwich Village church one winter afternoon, she is dressed in batik-print pants and dramatic bracelets. But what really catches one's attention is the large amulet-shaped necklace around Isaac's neck. It is one of the many jewelry pieces that Isaac has designed.

Even when Isaac smiles, her large eyes are sorrowful, accentuated by her closely cropped black hair. Asked by a student why she always wears a tiny gold earring shaped like a dancing figure, she answers, "That's my intuition. It's like a little angel so I'll do the right thing."

These days, forty-seven-year-old Isaac makes a concerted effort to listen to her intuition when it comes to her relationships with men. Her ex-boyfriend has just been sentenced to seven years in prison for setting fire to her apartment, the culmination of months of beatings and threats on her life.

Looking back, Isaac now sees her convicted boyfriend as part of a chain of abusive relationships. She thinks her own childhood with a violent father helps explain why she gravitated toward abusive men. Her father didn't just beat her. "He was constantly telling me: 'Get out of my sight, you're good for nothing,' " Isaac remembers. "These are tapes that, as an adult, play back in my head and, of course, give me a very low self-esteem."

When Isaac was nine years old, her father herded her, her three siblings, and their mother into a room and told them he was going to kill them. They managed to escape. Isaac's father was arrested and sent to a mental institution. Unfortunately, the bad news didn't end there. When Isaac was twelve, her mother was murdered. Although the crime was never solved, Isaac believes the murderer was an abusive boyfriend her mother became involved with after her father's breakdown. Isaac spent her teenage years living in foster homes.

Isaac's bad experiences seemed far away when, in the spring of 1998, she met a man named Lorenzo at a flea market. She remembers him coming up to a booth where she was selling jewelry. She was surrounded by a bevy of female friends and relatives. "I felt special that he wanted my phone number," she says.

Isaac and Lorenzo became romantically involved, and he soon moved in with her. The good times did not last long. Within a couple of months, Lorenzo had lost his job, was getting high, and was demanding money from Isaac. He began to exhibit a violent side. The first time she refused him money, he tried to smother her with a pillow. On another occasion, he threatened her with a machete.

"He would sling me around, smack me," Isaac remembers. But Isaac never called the police. Lorenzo played on her fears. Knowing of her mother's violent death, he would tell Isaac, "You're going to die just like your mother died."

Several times, Isaac came close to breaking off with Lorenzo. It never lasted long. Aside from fear, what held Isaac back from a permanent break-up was Lorenzo's remorseful behavior in between his violent episodes—a cycle typical of abusive relationships. "He was very loving, a totally different person," says Isaac. "He would promise me he would get help, he wouldn't drink."

Despite Lorenzo's promises, the abuse continued. Finally, Isaac told him she was leaving him for good and tried to make a mad dash out of the apartment. He pinned her against the wall, but she managed to run to a neighbor's apartment downstairs, where she phoned the police. When Isaac accompanied the cops to her apartment to look for Lorenzo, flames leapt out of the doorway. Lorenzo had already left. He was arrested later that evening on an arson charge.

Lorenzo's destruction of Pamela Isaac's home was an act of revenge: "Because I ran away from him, he was saying, 'I'm going to show her.'" The fire had a devastating effect on Isaac. Twenty-one years' worth of possessions were ruined. The landlord refused to let her move back to the building. In a flash, she had lost the home where she had spent most of her adult life.

For months, Isaac was forced to live in a homeless shelter. Humiliated and emotionally vulnerable, she quit her part-time job teaching crafts at a nursing home. "It was very painful. I cried a lot. I was a nervous wreck," Isaac says of that period.

So Isaac was surprised by what she found when she arrived at the Brooklyn District Attorney's office. She had come as a witness to answer questions as prosecutors prepared a case against Lorenzo. Isaac was told that the case was being assigned to the Brooklyn Domestic Violence Court. A single judge and a single prosecutor—both specially trained in domestic violence—would be handling the case. As part of the process, Isaac was offered the assistance of a social worker to help her craft a safety plan and get back on her feet.

Still homeless, Isaac was provided with a voice mailbox so that she could pick up phone messages from prospective employers. The social worker also helped Isaac find a permanent apartment in subsidized housing—in a new neighborhood where Lorenzo would be less likely to find her. Isaac was also linked to weekly therapy sessions at the court building. "I don't think I would have gotten through this if I didn't have the help," Isaac says. "They didn't make me feel bad or stupid. Through the help of the court system, I was able to take time for myself and be kind to myself."

Even though Lorenzo was in jail awaiting trial, Isaac was worried that some of his relatives would try to hurt her in retaliation. She was reassured when the judge issued an order of protection, forbidding Lorenzo or any of his family members from contacting her while the case was pending.

When the case finally went to trial, Isaac told her social worker that she was again feeling overwhelmed with fear and was suffering physical symptoms from the anxiety. Because Lorenzo had threatened her family in the past, Isaac was afraid to let any of her relatives accompany her to court. So both the therapist and the social worker sat beside her during the trial and held her hands as she sat disguised in a blond wig and dark glasses.

"She used a disguise because she was so afraid of the defendant," remembers Assistant District Attorney Cynthia Lynch, who prosecuted the case. At Isaac's request, Lynch escorted her outside and sent her home in a cab after each trial session.

At the trial, Lorenzo contended that the fire had been caused by a cooking accident. In his statement, he turned on the old charm, claiming that he was a joint partner with Isaac in her jewelry business, that they loved one another, and that he would never try to hurt her.

In response, Assistant District Attorney Lynch contended that Lorenzo had a motive for the arson: He was about to be thrown out of the apartment, losing both his shelter and his girlfriend's financial support. "When I was assigned the case, I didn't see it as just arson," explains Lynch, who specializes in domestic-violence cases. "There was an assault involved. There was some really nasty behavior before he set the place on fire. There was that motive: 'I'm losing my meal ticket.' That's not necessarily a picture that would be presented if the case weren't handled in domestic-violence court."

Some other problem-solving courts require that defendants affirmatively choose the problem-solving forum over prosecution in a conventional courtroom. Most defendants are happy to make this choice, since it brings with it the prospect that they will avoid jail if they successfully fulfill the court's requirements. This is not the case with domestic-violence courts, which are in the business of trying to stiffen penalties for batterers.

Indeed, in cases like Lorenzo's, the DA's domestic-violence unit makes a concerted effort to piece together the history of domestic violence that contributed to the crime. "In Brooklyn, the domestic-violence-court judge has extensive training [in domestic violence] and is receptive to the particular history that comes with a victim," says Lynch.

Isaac testified that Lorenzo never contributed to any of the household bills while he lived with her but that she continued to give him money because she was afraid of him. She told the court about Lorenzo's threat that she would die just like her mother. She testified that she was so afraid of Lorenzo that she had changed the locks on her door. She described his "Dr. Jekyll and Mr. Hyde" personality, which vacillated between violent behavior and loving apologies.

In January 2003, Lorenzo pled guilty to attempted arson and received a sentence of seven years in prison. The court also issued an order of protection forbidding any contact between Lorenzo and Isaac until 2013.

Unlike conventional courts, where a victim might have had to tell her story to a new prosecutor at every step of the way, from indictment to trial to appeal, the Brooklyn Domestic Violence Court—with the support of innovative Brooklyn District Attorney Charles J. Hynes—allowed the same prosecutor and judge to handle the case throughout, minimizing the possible trauma. Many victims report that they have been victimized twice—once by the perpetrator of the crime and then again by an insensitive criminal justice system. The Court's familiarity with Isaac's case and her emotional state ensured this didn't happen.

The prosecutor's office continues to stay in touch with Isaac to this day. "We don't disappear just because the trial is over," Lynch says. When the date approaches for Lorenzo's release or parole, the DA's office will notify Pamela so that she can make plans to ensure her safety, including moving to a new address if necessary.

With the help of therapy and a domestic-violence support group, Isaac says she has gained a new understanding of why she was drawn to abusive men in the first place. "I was looking for validation, for love because I was abandoned" as a child, she says. Today, she says, she finds that validation elsewhere—through her artwork and through friends she has made at her church. "I feel different. I act different. I haven't attracted any more losers," Isaac maintains.

On a recent evening, Pamela worked at her church as a volunteer, smiling and joking with fellow congregants as she served dinner to AIDS patients. She is currently involved with a man who has a sense of self-sufficiency that her former boyfriends lacked. "He has his own apartment, a way of making a living. He's not dependent and he's not violent," Isaac reports.

"She's come a long way," Prosecutor Lynch affirms. After the arson, "she had a bit of enlightenment, some insight. She was willing to examine, 'How could I have been with this man?' and to say, 'I need to protect myself and make sure it doesn't happen with someone else.' "

Since the trial, Isaac has become an outspoken advocate for domestic-violence victims. She has spoken publicly at conferences about her own situation and has led art workshops for domestic-violence victims. In 2000, she received an award from New York governor George Pataki, commending her for her courage.

Today, Isaac considers the public acknowledgment of domestic violence one of the Court's most valuable contributions—not only toward repairing her own life but also toward educating a broader audience. As a child, the abuse she suffered and witnessed against her mother "was a dirty little family secret," Isaac says. "Because of the help I got through the court system, it doesn't have to be a dirty little secret anymore."

6

Effectiveness: Do Problem-Solving Courts Work?[1]

What we have learned is that across the board,
the participants [in drug courts] are less likely
to be rearrested.
— ADELE HARRELL, The Urban Institute[2]

Any new idea is, and should be, subject to scrutiny. This is particularly true in a field like the law, where practitioners are professionally trained to be critics. Concerns about problem-solving courts generally fall into two broad categories— effectiveness and fairness. Carl Baar and Freda F. Solomon, in an essay titled, "The Role of Courts," describe "two faces of justice": One looks to preserve public order by controlling crime, and the other looks to protect individual rights by upholding due-process protections.[3] In this chapter and the one that follows, we review the record of problem-solving courts with regard to both preserving order and protecting rights. Because the problem-solving movement is still relatively young, the state of knowledge in the field changes on almost a daily basis, with a new evaluation or scholarly article being published nearly every week. These chapters are, of necessity, snapshots of a moving target.

In evaluating problem-solving courts, it is crucial to look at the context from which they have emerged. The relevant question is not just "What's the record of problem-solving courts?" but "How does that record compare to business as usual?" Are problem-solving courts any more or less effective at preserving public order than typical state courts? Does their use of coercion make a difference? Have they improved results for victims, neighborhoods, and defendants? Just as important, are problem-solving courts fair? How do they compare to standard case processing when it comes to preserving individual rights?

THIRTY YEARS OF FRUSTRATION

In 1974, a sociologist named Robert Martinson wrote an article for *The Public Interest* titled "What Works? Questions and Answers About Prison Reform." The article offered a bleak assessment of rehabilitation, concluding that, "With few and isolated exceptions, the rehabilitative efforts that have been reported so far have had no appreciable effect on recidivism."[4]

In many respects, Martinson's essay and the public debate it sparked cast a pall over the field of criminal justice for years. To this day, reformers find themselves grappling with the assumption, held by many academics, policy makers, and citizens, that "nothing works."

In 1996, University of Pennsylvania criminologist Lawrence Sherman confronted this mindset with his influential report, *Preventing Crime: What Works, What Doesn't, What's Promising*. He wrote,

Merely because a program has not been evaluated properly does not mean that it is failing to achieve its goals. Previous reviews of crime prevention programs, especially in prison rehabilitation, have made that error, with devastating consequences for further funding for those efforts. In addressing the unevaluated programs, we must blame the lack of documented effectiveness squarely on the evaluation process, and not on the programs themselves.[5]

Sherman infused a measure of hope into the field by throwing out the "nothing works" conclusion. But the more accurate conclusion that he offers in its place—that we still know very little about what works—comes with its own set of frustrations.

In general, criminal justice researchers face a political climate that prefers definitive answers to cautious preliminary findings, and is still likely to mistake uncertainty for proof of failure. Unfortunately, preliminary findings and qualified endorsements are often the best we have to work with. In truth, many criminal justice programs are not subject to any evaluation. While the demand for criminal justice research is high, both among policy makers and practitioners, the financial support is not. Outside of the National Institute of Justice at the U.S. Department of Justice (which has seen its budget dramatically reduced in recent years), there are few sources of funding for criminal justice research. This is a fact of life in criminal justice.

Beyond the difficulty of finding funding, problem-solving justice poses other challenges for researchers. First and foremost, it demands that researchers look beyond the usual measures of court effectiveness (How many cases were disposed? How fast? What were the dispositions?) to ask new questions about victims (How many were linked to services?

Are they any safer?), offenders (Have they changed their behavior? Have they gotten clean? Avoided further offending? Found a job?) and communities (How do citizens feel about the responsiveness of the courts? About the quality of life in their neighborhoods?). In short, problem-solving courts dramatically expand the scope of inquiry about the effectiveness of the justice system.

Moreover, the definition of success varies significantly from model to model. For example, in domestic-violence courts, the measures might be victim satisfaction, the percentage of offenders who comply with court orders, and the number of offenders who recidivate. In a community court, the relevant measures might be whether the court has changed sentencing practice (reducing short-term jail sentences and "walks" and increasing the use of alternative sanctions), how much community-service crews contribute to the neighborhood in labor each year, and what impact the project has had on levels of fear in the community. Meanwhile, drug courts look at not only whether offenders get clean and avoid crime, but also whether they get jobs, go to school, reunite with their families, and leave welfare. The one measure all the courts share is a desire to reduce repeat business. In one way or another, they all seek to change the behavior of offenders, preventing them from returning to court as recidivists.

 Despite these challenges, problem-solving courts have begun to leave a significant paper trail in recent years. A great many problem-solving courts have produced process and/or impact evaluations. Indeed, in the history of criminal justice innovation, it is difficult to locate many new ideas that have been better documented or researched than problem-solving courts.

What do we now know about problem-solving courts? How do we know it? After more than a decade of practice, what conclusions, if any, can be drawn about these judicial experiments? And where are the gaps in our knowledge? Which areas are ripe for further study? This chapter attempts to answer these questions.

DRUG COURT

Any review of problem-solving court research must begin with drug courts. Since 1989, when the first drug court opened, the model has been replicated widely. As a result, drug courts have generated a sizable body of research on their operations and outcomes. Drug courts now have enough of a track record to sustain an informed discussion of how they work, how well they work, and why they work.

Within the field of drug-court research, there is a growing consensus that drug courts reduce recidivism among participants even years after they leave the program. For example, a recent study of six New York drug courts—urban and rural, large and small—found that drug-court participants had an average reduction in recidivism of 29 percent—a significantly lower reconviction rate after three years than similar offenders who were prosecuted in conventional courtrooms.[6] Significantly, this comparison includes *both* program graduates and failures. If we were to look at only drug-court *graduates*, separating out those participants who ultimately fail treatment, the numbers are truly staggering: drug-court graduates recidivate 71 percent less than offenders who go through conventional courts.

Another recent study found that high-rate offenders—those with an average of twelve prior arrests and five prior convictions—who participated in the Baltimore Drug Court were 19 percent less likely to be re-arrested than comparable offenders three years after their original arrest. Because

subjects were randomly assigned to either drug court or conventional court, this study, by Denise Gottfredson of the University of Maryland, is the most methodologically rigorous
study of post-program effects to date.[7] Further, a literature
review of forty-one drug-court evaluations from across the
country revealed that thirty-five had achieved reduced recidivism, with an average difference in recidivism of 14 percent.[8]
The evidence is overwhelming: drug courts are one of the few
criminal justice interventions that have proven effective at
reducing criminal behavior.

Recidivism may be the most important measure, but
other indicators also show that the drug-court model makes
a difference. The research tells us that:

- *Offenders Mandated to Treatment Last Longer Than Other Clients.*
  Addicted offenders sentenced to court-mandated treatment
  are more than twice as likely to stay in treatment as individuals who pursue treatment voluntarily. The estimated
  national average one-year retention rate for mandatory
  treatment is 60 percent.[9] This means that at the end of one
  year, 60 percent of mandated offenders will still be in treatment. By way of contrast, reported retention rates for voluntary treatment programs range from 10 to 30 percent
  over a one-year period.[10] Interestingly, this statistic runs
  counter to the conventional wisdom that motivation for
  self-improvement has to come from within an individual
  rather than from external forces. The research suggests that
  the use of coercive authority in problem-solving courts can
  make a life-changing difference for offenders.

- *Treatment Changes Behavior.* The longer participants stay in
  treatment, the better the outcomes. A study of an Oregon
  program demonstrated that even people who ultimately

dropped out of treatment were less likely to be re-arrested if they'd stayed in for at least ninety days.[11] This finding points to the importance of looking beyond what happens to graduates of drug courts; outcomes for other participants (even those who "fail" in treatment) can be substantial and are worth studying.[12]

- *Judicial Monitoring Makes a Difference.* Even absent treatment, sanctions can have a statistically significant impact on offenders' behavior. An Urban Institute study suggests that ongoing monitoring and the use of graduated sanctions and rewards can help drug offenders avoid re-arrest in the year after sentencing *even if offenders are not linked to treatment.*[13] Criminal justice researchers look at the effects of punishment in terms of certainty (whether the sanction will be enforced), severity (how harsh the sanction will be), and celerity (how quickly the sanction will be imposed). A recent study by Adele Harrell of the Urban Institute compared the graduated-sanctions programs in three drug courts and found that the severity of the sanctions had the greatest effect across the board on changing the behavior of offenders.[14] Again, coercion seems to make a difference.

- *Drug Courts Save Money.* Cost analyses reveal that drug courts save money when compared to traditional adjudication. For example, a Multnomah County, Oregon, study reports that for every dollar spent on drug court, the system saves $2.50 in avoided costs of conventional adjudication: This figure excludes costs related to victimization, theft reduction, public assistance, and medical claims. When those costs are added in, the savings reach $10 for every $1 spent.[15] On balance, the savings from reduced crime exceed the costs of running drug courts. A recent review reports that the savings from crime reduction (stemming from reduced recidivism) averages $2.83 for every dollar invested in drug courts.[16]

- *Drug Courts Have Other Beneficial Impacts.* According to the Department of Justice, more than 2,100 drug-free babies have been born to mothers while they were in drug-court programs.[17] Meanwhile, a survey of graduates in nine New York drug courts found that participants were significantly more likely to be employed at graduation than at program entry (the employment rate was 35 percent higher on average at graduation).[18] There are other intangible benefits to society from drug courts that are harder to calculate. These benefits include increased government revenues from personal income tax as addicts become taxpayers, reduced public-welfare costs, and reduced hospitalization costs. One of the biggest difficulties facing court administrators, however, is that savings of this kind often show up on the ledger of someone else—such as the Internal Revenue Service or the state welfare agency—rather than as savings to the court system.

Based on these and other findings, there is a growing consensus among criminal justice officials that drug courts have indeed proven to be an effective intervention. Assistant Attorney General Deborah Daniels, the head of the Office of Justice Programs for the Bush administration, summed up the feelings of many when she flatly declared: "Drug courts work."[19]

DOMESTIC-VIOLENCE COURT

The primary objective of most domestic-violence courts is the enhancement of victim safety. Other outcome measures include reduced recidivism, improved monitoring and accountability for defendants, improved case-processing efficiency, and better coordination among all of the players involved in domestic-violence cases.

As yet, there have been few rigorous evaluations of domestic-violence courts. Most research to date takes the form of process evaluations rather than experimental studies. An Urban Institute study of the Brooklyn Felony Domestic Violence Court, for example, pointed to some significant procedural improvements.[20] The study revealed improved coordination among stakeholders both inside and outside the court system: thanks to the domestic-violence court, lawyers, judges, and representatives from victims' services and batterer programs started meeting together for the first time. Victim advocates were assigned to 100 percent of the victims who came through the court, up from 55 percent under the old system. Among defendants released on bail, 44 percent were sent to batterer programs (up from zero). Before the specialized court opened, 73 percent of domestic-violence felony defendants entered a guilty plea; after, 88 percent entered guilty pleas.

Another Urban Institute study found that a domestic-violence court in Shelby County, Tennessee, cut case dismissals in half, and that a court in Lexington County, South Carolina, significantly reduced the rearrest rate of misdemeanor offenders in the eighteen months after initial arrest. Perhaps unsurprisingly, 76 percent of the victims in the South Carolina court rated case handling as excellent or good.[21] Given the revictimization that many victims experience when they come to court, these numbers are remarkable.

While these studies of domestic-violence courts are promising, most of what we know about the effectiveness of the domestic-violence-court model derives from studies of the model's core components—particularly batterer-intervention programs, judicial monitoring, and orders of protection—within the context of regular criminal court. For example, batterer-intervention programs (essentially reeducation programs that give an overview of the history and context of domestic violence) are widely used in conventional criminal courts as a sanction for batterers.[22]

Batterer-intervention programs are popular, but how well do they work? A literature review conducted by Larry W. Bennett and Oliver J. Williams cites three measures for a program's success: "(1) Are batterers held accountable for their crime (or, has justice been served)? (2) Are victims safe? And, (3) Has the batterer changed his attitudes and behavior?"[23] The authors reach two conclusions: "(1) Batterers programs as currently configured have modest but positive effects on violence prevention, and (2) there is little evidence at present supporting the effectiveness of one batterers intervention program approach over another." This may change soon. There is significant interest in the research community in looking at different types of batterer programs (the Deluth reeducation model has dominated the field in the past but now faces competition from other emerging models). The next few years may yield much more information on this topic.

The available evidence suggests that rigorous court monitoring—requiring defendants to return to court regularly to report on their compliance with court orders—may have more of an effect on recidivism than batterer-reeducation programs. Most telling in this regard is a recent random assignment experiment in Brooklyn, which compared offenders assigned to community service to those linked to batterer-intervention programs.[24] There were three experimental groups: one community-service track; one twenty-six-week batterer-intervention-program track; and one eight-week batterer-intervention-program track (while the length of the programs was considerably different, the total number of hours required of participants was the same).

Perhaps predictably, more participants successfully completed the eight-week program than the twenty-six-week program; however, only participants in the twenty-six-week program exhibited lower violence rates than those of the community-service group. Neither group provided evidence that participants had learned anything as a result of their treatment, but the ones least likely to reabuse were those who were under court supervision for the longest period of time. In other words, judicial monitoring, not batterer-intervention, seemed to have made the difference in promoting victim safety. This is pretty strong evidence to suggest that the emphasis that problem-solving courts place on judicial involvement over the long haul is well founded.

Two other studies are worthy of note here. In 2000, San Diego court administrators conducted an internal study that underlined the importance of judicial monitoring by showing that the highest rates of recidivism in domestic-violence cases took place between arrest and case disposition. In the first year, with only a batterer program in place, recidivism was at 21 percent; the next year, when the court added a judicial monitoring component, recidivism dropped to 14 percent.[25]

A 1997 study of two projects in Milwaukee examined the effects of two sequential changes in the court system with respect to domestic-violence cases: first, the establishment of a specialized court; second, a change in the district attorney's screening policy that increased the pool of cases heard in the domestic-violence court to include many with uncooperative victims. The creation of the specialized court resulted in a 50 percent reduction in case-processing time, a 25 percent increase in convictions, and a decline in pre-trial crime. By contrast, the change in prosecutorial policy caused a case backlog, a decline in convictions, an increase in pretrial crime, and lower levels of victim satisfaction.

Researchers drew the following implications: shortening court-processing time in domestic-violence cases is a good idea; introducing domestic-violence cases with reluctant victims into the criminal justice system should be carefully considered, and undertaken only with sufficient resources for prosecution and adjudication; and in deciding whether or not to prosecute, the victim's voice should be taken into account. [26]

Victims present some distinct challenges for domestic-violence-court researchers. Police and court records may not indicate how much abuse has actually occurred, and victims, if they are involved in the court process at all, are often reluctant to participate in formal studies.

A recent study of a specialized domestic-violence court in Toronto revealed that a case was seven times more likely to be prosecuted if the victim was perceived as cooperative, even in a court specifically designed to minimize reliance on victim cooperation.[27] Meanwhile, a 1993 study of a domestic-violence prosecution program in Indianapolis that examined several different prosecutorial policies found significant rates of continued abuse, regardless of prosecutorial policy. Interestingly, the victims in the greatest jeopardy were those who dropped charges after the batterer was summoned to court. The researchers concluded that "Prosecutors can help victims minimize the chance of violence by affirming the legitimacy of their criminal complaints and by respecting their decisions about what is best under their unique circumstances, even if contrary to the prosecutor's administrative concerns."[28] (Other research qualifies the above findings by indicating that mandatory-arrest policies do result in a net reduction in domestic-violence offenses, regardless of how the victim participates in the process.)[29]

A pending experiment in the Bronx seeks to explore the relative effectiveness of judicial monitoring and batterer-intervention programs as responses to misdemeanor domestic violence. Convicted batters in the Bronx will be divided at random into four 200-person test groups. One group will participate in a batterer-intervention program and receive monthly monitoring; a second group will participate in a batterer program and receive court monitoring on a graduated schedule; a third group will not participate in a batterer program but will receive monthly monitoring; and a fourth group will not participate in a batterer program or receive graduated monitoring. This study, scheduled to conclude in 2005, presents an opportunity to simultaneously test two components of the specialized-court model—batterer programs and court monitoring—under experimental conditions. When it is completed, we will know a lot more than we do today about fashioning an effective response to domestic violence.

COMMUNITY COURT

Community courts present special challenges to researchers. Because each court seeks to respond to the unique nature of its home community, there are multiple community-court models. And because they often aspire to achieve goals beyond the narrowly defined world of criminal justice (e.g., improvements in public confidence in justice and in communication among neighborhood agencies), community courts require more ambitious research designs.

The most extensive evaluation of a community court to date is the National Center for State Courts' study of the

Midtown Community Court, which compared the Community Court's sentences and defendants' compliance rates to
a sample of defendants from Manhattan's centralized,
downtown court. [30] Findings include:

- *Changes in Sentencing Practice.* The Midtown Community Court
  substantially changed sentencing practice for low-level
  offenses, by imposing more community-service and social-
  service sentences: "The Midtown Community Court makes
  much greater use of intermediate sanctions (81% of disposed
  cases) than the Downtown Court (31% of disposed cases)."[31]

- *Reduced "Walks."* Offenders sentenced at Midtown were far
  less likely than those downtown to walk out of court without any punishment for charges like prostitution, drug
  possession, and turnstile jumping: "One consequence of the
  new Court's commitment to using intermediate sanctions
  is a reduction in the frequency of sentences in which no
  conditions are imposed. . . . In the aggregate, substantially
  more cases receive such sentences Downtown (47%) than at
  Midtown (10%)."[32]

- *Reduced Use of Short-Term Jail Sentences.* At the same time, Midtown reduced the use of jail sentences of less than five days:
  "Jail sentences represented a substantially higher proportion of arraignment sentences Downtown (18%) than at
  Midtown (8%)."[33]

- *Improved Compliance with Court Orders.* Offenders were also
  significantly more likely to comply with their community-
  service sentences at Midtown: "There is clear evidence that
  aggregate community service compliance rates are higher
  at Midtown than Downtown (75 percent compared to 50
  percent)."[34]

- *Reductions in Street Crime.* As for the impact on the neighbor-hood, researchers found prostitution and unlicensed vending, two major community problems, dropped significantly over the first eighteen months: ". . . The volume of arrests for street prostitution in Midtown began dropping dramatically when the Midtown Community Court opened, and continued to drop throughout the research period—a 56 percent decline compared to a comparable baseline period."[35] Community residents also reported a marked reduction in graffiti.

A followup evaluation found continued improvements in the neighborhood's quality of life, with prostitution markets declining even further in the Court's second and third years. Among Midtown's residential and business communities, there was general agreement that the Midtown Court had contributed to improvements in the area.[36]

Researchers also analyzed the project's costs and benefits. They quantified significant cost savings in the following areas: shortened arrest-to-arraignment times, reduced use of jail, and the value of clean-up work by community-service work crews. According to the evaluators, "the net jail saving of the project over three years was . . . roughly 12,600 jail days—or approximately 35 jail years."[37] (Portland's community courts are also expected to save a significant number of jail days. For Portland's Westside community court alone, the district attorney's office estimates a $95,000 savings in the course of a year as a result of 820 jail days saved.) [38]

On the cost side of the ledger, Midtown's evaluators quantified the expenses associated with computer equipment, overhead, and construction. Most of the extra costs went to support new staff positions, such as social workers and community-service supervisors.

While these hard costs were easy to quantify, researchers could not determine with precision whether the value of benefits exceeded costs during Midtown's start-up period, in large part because they had difficulty putting a price on the "intangible" costs and benefits of the Midtown experiment. They concluded: "It is likely that the dollar value of unmeasured benefits (e.g., improved quality of life in Midtown, reduced recidivism for those who complete drug treatment) is greater than the dollar value of unmeasured 'add-on' costs (e.g., lost economies of scale in criminal justice agencies; larger than typical staffing levels)."[39]

PUBLIC PERCEPTIONS

While problem-solving courts are designed to improve case processing and court outcomes, they also seek to make an impact in the world of public opinion. How are these courts perceived by relevant stakeholders? Do they improve public confidence in justice?

Recent surveys conducted by the National Center for State Courts have attempted to document public attitudes toward problem-solving courts. These surveys demonstrate that while the public may not know what a problem-solving court is per se, they share problem-solving court innovators' concerns about revolving-door justice. The research also indicates high levels of public support for basic problem-solving methods.

For example, a 2001 survey found strong support, particularly among African American and Hispanic respondents, for common problem-solving strategies, including the hiring of treatment staff and social workers, bringing offenders back to court to report on their progress in treatment, coordinating the work of local treatment agencies to help offenders, and bringing in relevant outside experts to help courts make more informed decisions. The report concluded:

> A solid majority of the public backs new court and judicial roles associated with problem-solving. . . . Support for these new roles is strongest among African-Americans and Latinos. For example, more than 80 percent of those groups support courts hiring counselors and social workers. . . . The highly positive response of African-Americans to changes that would increase the involvement of the courts in people's lives is a marked contrast with the negative views African-Americans generally have of judges and the courts.[40]

What do judges think of problem-solving courts? A study of state court judges conducted by the University of Maryland suggested that the judiciary shares the public's endorsement of basic problem-solving tools.[41] More than 500 criminal court judges were surveyed. Participants supported treatment as an alternative to incarceration for addicted, nonviolent offenders (77 percent agreed that treatment was more effective than jail). They overwhelmingly agreed that the bench should be involved in reducing drug abuse among defendants (91 percent). And they also cited the need for more information about past violence when deciding bail and sentences in domestic-violence cases (90 percent agreed). Sixty-three percent of the judges surveyed said they should be more involved with community groups in addressing neighborhood safety and quality-of-life concerns. This runs counter to the popular assumption that judges are unwilling to engage with the community.

How do defendants perceive problem-solving courts? While no national survey has been undertaken, as part of the National Center for State Courts' evaluation of the Midtown

Community Court, researchers conducted individual interviews with defendants, who commented on the court's better facilities and faster case processing. Interestingly, they found the sentences meted out by the court *tougher* than those issued in conventional courts. But when asked which court they preferred, they chose Midtown. Why? They felt that Midtown personnel treated them better.

How do residents perceive problem-solving courts? A neighborhood survey of Midtown Manhattan revealed that the majority of residents (two-thirds) would be willing to pay more taxes to keep their community court in operation.[42] In Red Hook, Brooklyn, residents' approval ratings of the local community court stand in stark contrast to their historic distrust of the criminal justice system. A 2001 door-to-door survey conducted a year after the Red Hook Community Justice Center opened revealed that two out of every three local residents rated the Justice Center positively.[43] By contrast, in a survey conducted before the community court opened, only 12 percent of residents approved of the job that courts were doing in Brooklyn.[44] This suggests that, among other things, problem-solving courts could improve perceptions of justice.

A FUTURE RESEARCH AGENDA

Problem-solving courts have generated a growing body of research that documents solid results. By no means have researchers exhausted the potential questions for study, however. What follows is an attempt to define an agenda for the future of problem-solving-court research. It is intended to spark conversation rather than foreclose it. Inevitably, the most provocative questions will emerge at the local level—the product of a dynamic conversation between researchers and practitioners.

- *What Is the Active Ingredient?* Recognizing that complex problems call for complex solutions, problem-solving courts employ a vast array of ideas and strategies. It is worth isolating some of their core components, such as treatment, graduated sanctions, and judicial monitoring, to understand more precisely how the pieces within the problem-solving court model affect outcomes. What is the "active ingredient" in these experiments? To answer this question, it may make sense to look across projects—performing a comparative analysis, for example, of the role of the judge in drug courts, community courts, and domestic-violence courts.

- *Does It Work Over the Long Haul?* Researchers face tremendous challenges when they try to gather data about problem-solving court participants—particularly those who have left the programs due to either graduation or failure. If program dropouts or failures end up in jail, "post-program" only begins once they get out—which could be years from the original arrest that sent them to a problem-solving court in the first place. Many studies do not track what happens to participants who do not graduate from a problem-solving court but instead return to conventional adjudication. Nevertheless, post-program outcomes are vital to understanding the long-term effects of problem-solving courts—and how they compare to the effects of conventional practice.

- *Does Anything Matter Except Recidivism?* Unlike many criminal justice programs, problem-solving courts have not been shy about measuring the recidivism of participants. As important as recidivism is, there are a number of other potential impacts that bear investigation, particularly as problem-solving courts broaden their scope to include difficult populations with histories of mental illness and violence.

Graduation exit interviews can shed light on how participants' lives have changed since their first contact with the
court. Offenders who were homeless upon arrest may now
have a place to live; women who were pregnant and addicted
may have given birth to drug-free babies; people without high
school diplomas may have GEDs. Alternatively, participants
in long-term treatment may have lost their jobs or their mar-
riages while getting help for their addiction. There are potentially endless consequences—some intended, others not—that
might accrue from participating in a problem-solving court.
Studies can track these types of changes with relative ease
while defendants are under the court's control, but post-
program impacts are harder to assess.

- *Is Problem Solving Faster?* Given intense caseload pressures,
  state court systems are looking for ways to reduce backlogs
  and repeat appearances. Problem-solving courts may allevi-
  ate some of the burden on the conventional system by
  diverting certain types of offenders, but they also require
  more face time between defendant and judge, better tracking and record-keeping, and more administrative resources
  while the case is in the system. Do problem-solving courts
  speed up or slow down the administration of justice?

- *Can You Measure Coercion?* Problem-solving courts exert—or
  threaten to exert—legal force as part of their efforts to
  change the behavior of offenders. Some critics have argued
  that no one should be coerced into treatment. Others have
  wondered whether problem-solving courts diminish the
  ability of defense attorneys to engage in zealous advocacy
  on behalf of their clients. Advocates assert that problem-
  solving courts have done little to alter the practice of
  lawyering or the nature of due process but have simply

given attorneys and judges more tools to work with. It would be nice to bring some data to this debate. Future research could investigate whether problem-solving courts do indeed represent a change in the way defendants' rights are protected. This might include both qualitative work (how do defendants and their attorneys perceive procedural fairness in a problem-solving court?) and quantitative work (comparing the number of objections and plea bargains with those of a conventional court, for example).

- *Do Problem-Solving Courts "Widen the Net"?* Critics of problem-solving courts also voice unease about the effect of these courts on the actions of other players in the criminal justice system. Does the existence of a drug court lead police officers to make arrests they otherwise would not have made? Does judicial monitoring lengthen state involvement in defendants' lives? Is this necessarily a bad thing? More glibly, is there a "build it and they will come" phenomenon at work here? Having created problem-solving courts, will criminal justice agencies feel compelled to fill their caseloads by any means necessary? Research can help answer these questions by studying arrest patterns and prosecutorial and judicial decision making.

- *Do Better Courts Mean Stronger Neighborhoods?* In recent years, a number of new theories have been advanced to explain why some neighborhoods are safe, healthy, and economically viable and others are not. One of the key ideas running through this theoretical terrain is that strong communities promote information-sharing and coordination among civic institutions (whether they be churches, schools, or government agencies) and local residents. Because of their emphasis on interagency collaboration and public engagement, problem-solving courts hold out the possibility that they might contribute to the healthy functioning of the neighborhoods in which they reside. This idea is ripe for further exploration. Can community courts spur neighborhood revitalization? Does the coordination of services within the court lead to new levels of cooperation among community stakeholders beyond the courthouse? Can courts serve as a bridge between government and citizens? How might researchers document and assess this? These are questions that as yet have attracted little attention in the field.

It goes without saying that this chapter only pricks the surface of the possibilities for problem-solving-court research. The rapid proliferation of these experiments has been driven by more than just rhetoric or funding; it has been driven by the ability of problem-solving courts to generate demonstrable results, however provisional or inadequately studied. Framing a research agenda for problem-solving courts is much more than an academic exercise. It is of vital importance to the future of the problem-solving movement. If problem-solving courts hope to continue to thrive, and if they hope to move from the margins to the mainstream justice system, they must answer the concerns of critics and continue to win over the agnostics. The only way to do this is through rigorous, independent research that focuses on the questions that matter most to practitioners and policy makers.

7

Fairness: What Impact
Do Problem-Solving Courts Have
on Individual Rights?[1]

I think what you need at problem-solving courts
are attorneys, on both sides, who are willing to say,
"Judge, our normal procedure is not going
to work in this case," and then have the judge
make an independent decision.

—HON. KATHLEEN BLATZ, chief judge, State of Minnesota[2]

We now turn to the question of fairness. We start by acknowledging that the struggles of today's state courts to protect individual rights in the face of massive caseloads are well documented. As we discuss in chapter 1, the reality is that all too many criminal courts have become high-volume "plea-bargain mills," where the emphasis is on resolving the maximum number of cases in the minimum amount of time. In this overloaded environment, cases are resolved with insufficient regard to defendants' underlying problems or the impact of offending behavior on communities. Under these circumstances, it is reasonable to ask whether the status-quo courts effectively protect rights *or* promote public safety.

Have problem-solving courts altered the due-process protections found in today's criminal courts? What has their impact been on the adversarial process and the role of attorneys? Do they expose defendants to increased coercion? Do such courts widen the net of social control, bringing vulnerable populations (minorities, youth, homeless) into the criminal justice system that would not otherwise find themselves under the authority of the state? The pages that follow examine some of the hot-button issues that critics have raised about the fairness of problem-solving courts.

DO PROBLEM-SOLVING COURTS "WIDEN THE NET" OF SOCIAL CONTROL?

Critics have argued that problem-solving courts help bring into the criminal justice system individuals whose offenses would otherwise merit little attention. For example, Judge Morris Hoffman has argued that in Denver, Colorado, "The very presence of the drug court with its significantly increased capacity for processing cases has caused police to make arrests in, and prosecutors to file, the kinds of $10 and $20 hand-to-hand drug cases that the system simply would not have bothered with before, certainly not as felonies."[3]

In a similar vein, New York University law professor Anthony C. Thompson has argued that with community courts, the judicial system has assumed authority over conduct normally considered "beyond its mandate."[4] Thompson takes aim at the Midtown Community Court in particular, arguing that it "opened the door for police to increase the number of citations and arrests for low-level offenses."[5]

Put simply, there is no empirical evidence to support these claims. In Manhattan, the data show that misdemeanor arrests did indeed explode throughout the 1990s following the city's well-publicized crackdown on quality-of-life offenses.[6] But in Midtown Manhattan, home of the Midtown Community Court, the increase was no greater than in any other neighborhood. Indeed, Midtown experienced *less* of an increase than many city neighborhoods.

The Midtown Community Court may not bring more people into the system, but it does make sure that offenders receive a sentence of some kind.[7] As we have seen, getting a "walk"—a sentence of "time served" or a sentence with no condition imposed—is far less common at the community court than at Manhattan's conventional court downtown. For example, prostitutes are forty times less likely to receive walks at the Midtown Community Court than at the standard criminal court.[8]

Seen in this light, community courts are an exercise not in net widening but in net mending. The fact that so many convicted offenders walk away from criminal court without any meaningful response is a fundamental problem. When courts allow offenders to walk, when the process becomes the punishment, they send the wrong message to offenders, victims, police, and community residents. The message is that nobody cares, that the justice system is little more than a set of revolving doors.

DOES THE PUNISHMENT FIT THE CRIME AT PROBLEM-SOLVING COURTS?

The history of juvenile courts in the United States follows problem-solving courts around like a shadow.[9] As we discussed in chapter 2, it was not until decades after their inception, when a juvenile court judge sentenced a fifteen-year-old crank caller to a training school until adulthood, that the landmark Supreme Court case *In re Gault* introduced lawyers and due-process protections into the juvenile court process. Some critics have suggested that problem-solving courts could be heading down the same slippery slope, handing out harsh sentences in the name of rehabilitation and trampling individual rights in their zeal to solve defendants' problems.

"If you start with sensitivity, you may wind up with paternalism," warns professor Carl Baar.[10] James L. Nolan Jr., a sociologist at Williams College, worries that drug courts blur the distinction between punishment and treatment, subjecting participants to court mandates of indeterminate length, and requiring participants to waive basic constitutional rights in the bargain.[11] "Maybe it's good for a defendant to go into a problem-solving court and try not to get a criminal record," says Cait Clarke of the National Legal Aid and Defender Association. "But if the consequences are that when you fail treatment, the sanctions are much more serious and you serve a longer period of time or have a more serious felony on the record, those are huge consequences. So defense lawyers are concerned: If my client goes into a problem-solving court, will they get slammed even harder?"[12]

By and large, problem-solving courts have paid close attention to these kinds of concerns. The good problem-solving courts have not lost sight of proportionality. With the exception of domestic-violence courts, most problem-solving courts rely on defendants to opt into the program. For this reason, problem-solving courts must have a finely attuned sense of the local legal marketplace—to make sure that the deal they are offering defendants is reasonable enough to provide an incentive to participate. You won't find many first-time shoplifters getting sentenced to two years of inpatient drug treatment, for example. One reason why not is that the defense attorney is always in the room to say, "My client won't take this plea." In contrast to juvenile courts, where offenders often had no legal representation, a meaningful defense presence exists in most problem-solving courts. Indeed, the best ones have included public defenders in the planning process to hammer out solutions to due process and proportionality concerns ahead of time.

A recent study of Baltimore's drug court provides the best empirical evidence to date that problem-solving court participants do not face harsher punishment than they would receive in conventional courts. The study, which assigned two groups randomly to drug court or regular court, found that drug-court participants spent fewer days in jail.[13] Those in the conventional court group received the bulk of their jail days as part of their original sentence; drug-court participants received most of their jail days as sanctions for infractions of rules, such as failing a drug test or not attending a program. The Baltimore study provides evidence that drug courts are neither soft on crime nor overly punitive. Rather, it suggests that drug-court penalties are carefully tailored to fit the crime.

Adele Harrell, a researcher at the Urban Institute, points to another interesting finding from the Baltimore study: the fact that much of the jail time for drug-court participants was for failure to comply with the program, she asserts, "suggests that participants had a chance to control the penalties received."[14] There is evidence that suggests that this perception of control on the part of participants is an important part of the effectiveness of the drug-court model. In an earlier study of the Washington, D.C., drug court, Harrell found that participants "emphasized that the importance of knowing the rules and seeing them applied consistently and fairly was critical in their compliance with drug testing requirements."[15]

DO PROBLEM-SOLVING COURTS UNFAIRLY COERCE DEFENDANTS?

Coercion is an issue of particular concern for defense attorneys. According to Minnesota state public defender John Stuart, "The defense attorney [in drug court] could say [to his client], 'I know you feel the police didn't have the right to stop you and look in your pockets, and we can have a court hearing in six months. And between now and then, unfortunately, you'll be in jail. Or you can waive that right, plead guilty tomorrow, and go to treatment right away, and by X date you'll be done with your chemical-dependency treatment. *And* they'll get you a job.' What the defense lawyer has to offer is not any certainty [about winning a trial or a hearing on constitutional issues]. Naturally the guy will go to treatment."

Like many public defenders, Stuart believes something has been lost "if the court is set up to give a person a sweet deal provided they never question how the police operate." On the other hand, he concedes that most of the time when his lawyers litigate a constitutional issue, they lose.

Moreover, there's a larger reality to consider. The truth is that defendants exercise their constitutional right to a trial in less than 5 percent of cases. "Let's face it, in the traditional urban criminal justice system, defense lawyers don't have time to talk to their clients. You don't have time to investigate. You have completely coercive plea setups," says San Diego deputy district attorney Patrick McGrath.[16]

So the operative question is: Are problem-solving courts any more coercive than the standard state courts? One way of assessing that question is to ask whether disposition rates—the rates at which cases are resolved through plea bargaining rather than through trial—are any different at problem-solving courts than at standard criminal courts for comparable cases. If problem-solving courts were more coercive, one would expect to see higher (and quicker) disposition rates in these courtrooms, as defendants sacrificed their trial rights to avail themselves of treatment services in an effort to avoid convictions and jail time.

While no study to date has taken a rigorous look at this issue, researchers have found that disposition rates at the Midtown Community Court are comparable to those at Manhattan's centralized downtown court.[17] This suggests that the climate at problem-solving courts may be no more or less coercive than the climate at many contemporary criminal courts.

At the end of the day, the primary difference may not be the amount of coercion but the purposes for which it is wielded. As New York judge Judy Harris Kluger has noted, "As it stands, many defendants are being pressured to take dispositions [like jail] that don't ultimately do anything to help them. If we are going to have to apply that kind of pressure, isn't it better that the pressure is in a life-changing direction—toward services and treatment that can make a difference?"[18]

In fact, problem-solving courts have the potential to improve upon the current climate of coercion. For example, problem-solving courts in Seattle and Portland have instituted structures that give defendants two weeks to test out treatment while their case is pending.[19] Defendants can use this period to opt into (or out of) treatment, while their defense attorneys can use the time to investigate the strength of the cases against their clients. Some problem-solving courts have arranged for open file discovery before taking a plea, in an effort to give defendants and their advocates a chance to assess the cases against them as quickly as possible. Still others have engaged in yearlong planning processes where rules and procedures have been hammered out in advance by both prosecutors and defenders—often in an adversarial climate.[20]

WHAT IMPACT DO PROBLEM-SOLVING COURTS HAVE ON THE ADVERSARIAL PROCESS?

Some critics ask whether the culture of team collaboration fostered in many problem-solving courts could have an insidious effect on attorneys' ability to engage in zealous advocacy. The role of the defense attorney is of particular concern to these critics.[21] "I'm concerned about the impact of telling the judge, the prosecutor and the defender that they are all in this little boat together and they have to get along out there on the ocean," says Stuart. "That, I think, could have a deleterious effect on the zealous advocacy of the defense attorney."[22]

Critics who have expressed concerns about adversarialism in problem-solving courts often point to drug courts, where after a defendant enters a guilty plea and opts into the program, all of the court players—judge, defender, and prosecutor—work together as a team to promote success in treatment.

This does not, however, mean that adversarialism is not alive and well in these courts. On the contrary, throughout the adjudication process—up until a defendant decides to plead guilty and enter treatment—prosecutors and defenders relate to one another (and the judge) much as they always have: as adversaries.

As researcher John Goldkamp has observed: "Generally adversarial procedures are employed at the screening and admission stage and at the conclusion of the drug court when participants are terminated and face legal consequences or graduate."[23] In other words, up until a defendant pleads guilty, a drug court looks pretty much like any other courtroom. It is a defense attorney's job to figure out whether participation in drug court makes sense for her client or whether the client is better off facing conventional prosecution. And it is a defense attorney's job to advocate for the best possible deal for her client within the confines of the pre-established drug-court rules and procedures.

Ironically, in some respects there may be *more* lawyering in drug courts than in comparable state courtrooms, where plea bargains are routine and the going rates are well known to all players. In addition to contesting the merits of each case, advocates in many drug courts also engage in policy arguments in the planning stages of the court, hashing out eligibility criteria, the length of treatment services, and appropriate treatment modalities (for example, outpatient versus residential).

In addition, lawyers in drug courts stay involved in a case over the long haul. In conventional courts, lawyers and judges typically step aside after a sentence is imposed. The job of overseeing offenders' compliance with court mandates is generally left to others (mostly to probation departments or jailers) or, in all too many cases, to no one. In contrast, problem-solving courts represent a shift in accountability—in these courtrooms, judges and lawyers have come to see the ongoing monitoring of offenders as a fundamental part of their jobs. As a result, the roles of prosecutors, defenders, and judges are often not confined to adjudication. Rather, they stay involved with each case throughout the sentencing process to monitor compliance.

Even in the post-adjudicative stage, however, there are bound to be objections from defenders. There is no doubt that problem-solving courts evoke an almost palpable ambivalence on the part of defense attorneys, who must navigate the tensions between teamwork and advocacy, between being part of a collaborative problem-solving enterprise and zealously defending the interests of their clients.[24]

Many problem-solving courts have successfully navigated this tension, creating space for defenders to advocate when necessary and to be part of the team when it is in the best interests of their clients. Most problem-solving courts are essentially voluntary—defendants can choose to opt out of them and face conventional prosecution. More fundamentally, problem-solving courts force defenders to think deeply about the best interests of their clients. Is it in the best interests of the client to walk out of court without receiving help when the lawyer knows that his client is just going to keep cycling through the system again and again? Problem-solving courts give defenders an opportunity to think about the long-term life trajectories of their clients—and hopefully to make a difference.

Indeed, defenders have been lobbying judges since time immemorial for treatment for clients. "I've been standing there for seventeen years begging judges to give people a drug program," says Lisa Schreibersdorf, executive director of the Brooklyn Defender Services in New York City. Problem-solving courts actually seek to deliver treatment, but with a price—greater state involvement in defendants' lives. It's the responsibility of defense attorneys to weigh these issues and help their clients make informed decisions.

The reality is that problem-solving courts, like all other courts, are fundamentally collaborative enterprises that require the active participation of prosecutors, judges, and defenders if they are going to work. Defense attorneys and their clients could effectively shut down drug courts by refusing to participate. But by and large, this hasn't happened.

Why not? One answer can be found in a letter to the edi-

tor by Daniel Greenberg, at the time head of the Legal Aid
Society in New York City, arguing on behalf of judge-driven
alternative-to-incarceration programs:

> Common sense tells us we are all better served when
> accused criminal defendants with addiction problems are
> treated rather than incarcerated for unconscionably long
> periods. . . . The Legal Aid Society has supported effective
> alternative to incarceration programs and we hope that
> their success will expand the willingness of others to use
> them. . . . We believe that greater promise of fairness and
> success lies with returning discretion to judges to fashion
> appropriate remedies and programs.[25]

While Greenberg's letter is not emblematic of widespread
excitement for problem-solving courts within the defense
bar, it is indicative of a growing sense of acceptance and
even endorsement among many defense attorneys. Defense
attorneys have expressed support, however conditional, for
problem-solving courts for a number of reasons. First and
foremost, it is because most problem-solving courts have
delivered what defenders have wanted from courts for
years—treatment for their clients—and have done it without
losing sight of the need for proportionality. Just as important, the good problem-solving courts have included defenders in the planning process, giving them a seat at the table
when determining eligibility criteria, treatment mandates,
and sanctioning schemes.

WHAT ABOUT DOMESTIC-VIOLENCE COURTS?

Problem-solving courts that deal with domestic violence
operate in a very different arena from other courts in this
new movement, and raise entirely different issues vis-à-vis

fairness and equity.[26] Domestic-violence courts are focused
not on rehabilitation of the defendant but rather on services
to the victim. These courts handle the most serious cases in
the problem-solving universe, including murders. These are
not "feel-good" courts. In contrast to a drug court, there are
no heart-warming graduation ceremonies in domestic-
violence court. In fact, many domestic-violence advocates wonder whether domestic-violence courts should even be called
problem-solving courts, because they think that implies that
an effective therapeutic response exists for battering.

What are the principal criticisms of domestic-violence
courts? First and foremost is the issue of fairness to defendants: "The creation of the Dade County Domestic Violence
Court . . . made it particularly difficult for the judges hearing cases of alleged domestic violence to operate as impartial, disinterested adjudicators," charges Miami public
defender Bennett H. Brummer.[27]

In most cases, the judge assigned to a domestic-violence
court has received special training in the nature of domestic violence, including such aspects as the cyclical nature
of domestic violence and behaviors by batterers that typically predict future violent acts. Court-sponsored training
sessions have been criticized by defense attorneys as "very
victim-oriented, ignoring the defendant's perspective."[28]
Indeed, some defense attorneys argue that by supplying
special victim advocates and a raft of services to the victim,
the court is tipping the scales, both symbolically and con-
cretely, against the defendant.

In response to defense attorneys' objections, some courts
have made special efforts to address any appearance of bias.
In Brooklyn, for example, court officials removed all signage
advertising the court as a "domestic-violence court" from the
courtroom for fear that it appeared to prejudge defendants.

More fundamentally, domestic-violence advocates argue that domestic-violence courts are helping to balance a system that has for too many years failed to take domestic violence seriously. Indeed, they have argued that domestic-violence courts have essentially leveled a playing field that has long favored defendants. Seen in this light, domestic-violence courts are an effort to account for the special nature of domestic-violence cases, which typically include a targeted victim, ongoing patterns of intimidation, and a relationship marked by economic dependence.

Nancy Greenberg, a prosecutor in the Brooklyn district attorney's office, recalls, "Before the domestic-violence court was in effect, every time a domestic-violence case was called, there was one judge who would say to the defendant 'Be nice to the little lady, buy her some chocolate, some flowers.'" The creation of a specialized court with trained judges at the bench "doesn't mean we always win," Greenberg emphasizes. "But we don't have to reinvent the wheel, start at square one with case law and with the same issues. The judges are attuned to what men can do in these relationships. They understand that stalking and those harassing phone calls can truly be affecting a woman's life—that she may have to change her job or move away."[29]

DOES PROBLEM-SOLVING JUSTICE THREATEN JUDICIAL IMPARTIALITY OR INDEPENDENCE?

In addition to asking hard questions about domestic-violence courts, some critics have queried whether problem-solving courts compromise judges' ability to render impartial, independent judgment. As judges become more acquainted with community residents through attending neighborhood meetings, are they able to hear cases fairly?

One answer to this can be found in the division of labor at the Midtown Community Court. While the Court is located in the community and was explicitly created with the idea of helping judges to understand the neighborhood impacts of chronic, low-level offending, it does not ask the judge to manage community relations. Instead, the Court charges administrative staff with this responsibility.

Nonetheless, the Court's decision to create a community advisory board—and have the sitting judge attend its meetings—made some local judges uneasy. Would the advisory board seek to second-guess judicial decisions? Would an advisory role lead inexorably to vigilante justice, to neighborhood activists making sentencing decisions? This has not been the case. The members of the advisory board, while actively engaged in thinking about the Court's programs and community-service projects, have never tried to lobby the judge about individual cases. Rather, they have been a valuable resource for the Court, helping to expand the array of community-service options and create post-disposition opportunities such as job training.

The truth is that too often judicial independence is used as an excuse for judicial ignorance. At the Red Hook Community Justice Center, Judge Alex Calabrese frequently attends community meetings, where he hears residents' complaints about the quality-of-life issues that bother them most. He is a well-known figure in the neighborhood and knows many of the residents by name. Does that hinder his ability to render an impartial judgment if a resident he knows appears before him in court? How is Calabrese's familiarity with local residents different from the experience of a judge in a small town?

While Calabrese reserves the right to send cases to another court if there is even an appearance of conflict, it is an option that he uses infrequently. "I think it's appropriate for a judge to learn about the community," he says. "I don't think you have to be completely blind to community issues to be fair. And in fact I think you're more effective if you know what the community problems are."[30] The bottom line for judges like Calabrese is that when judges are in the dark about how a neighborhood is affected by crime, it hinders their ability to make good decisions.

A trip to Calabrese's courtroom suggests that he has been able to balance a problem-solving orientation with an emphasis on fairness and due process. Visitors to Red Hook are often surprised to discover that every defendant is represented by counsel and that the prosecution stands up on every case. On a typical day, the majority of the offenders who plead guilty to crimes like drug possession, shoplifting, and prostitution in Red Hook end up receiving alternative sanctions like community restitution, job training, or treatment rather than incarceration. The Red Hook Community Justice Center has in fact changed sentencing practice, reducing the use of short-term jail and increasing the use of community-based services and sanctions.

But a typical day in Red Hook also finds a handful of cases dismissed and a few others receiving jail sentences. What this suggests is that the problem-solving approach has not affected the judge's ability to weigh the merits of each case. On the contrary, a problem-solving court like the one in Red Hook gives judges and attorneys more options so they can provide more individualized justice to defendants.

Based on courts like Red Hook, a growing number of observers have determined that, in the words of public defender John Stuart, "it is possible to accommodate both trials and problem solving."[31] Hofstra Law School professor Eric Lane, in an essay titled, "Due Process and Problem-Solving

Courts," concluded, "with certain cautions, problem-solving judging and lawyering . . . need not be in conflict with due process standards."[32]

The bottom line is that if they are implemented correctly, problem-solving courts have the potential to improve not just the effectiveness of sentencing, but the fairness of case processing as well. The good problem-solving courts are already achieving this vision. The challenge is to make sure that all problem-solving courts are good ones.

CONCLUSION

The Future of Problem-Solving Justice

As recently as 2003, it was possible for scholars to write that there were a number of areas within criminal justice "in which tradition is too stubborn to yield, or thinking is too narrow, or conditions are too overcrowded, to allow for the prospect of reform in more than minimal ways. For example, the past thirty-five years of . . . criminal court processing . . . [has] produced none of the thinking or capabilities necessary to introduce significant basic change."[1]

It is important to keep this framing in mind when thinking about both the past and the future of problem-solving courts. Given the context out of which it emerged, the idea of problem-solving justice has come very far very fast. As this book attests, problem-solving justice is now being practiced in every state and endorsed by mainstream decision-makers. In the process, the judges and attorneys who have sparked this movement have demonstrated that it is in fact possible to achieve "significant basic change" within the judiciary.

But the revolution is far from over. There are still plenty of battles to be fought if problem solving is to become the norm, as opposed to the exception, within state courts. We must continue to test new applications of the problem-solving model, exploring different problems that might lend themselves to a problem-solving approach. And we must figure out how to "go to scale" with problem-solving justice, altering the DNA of state court systems so that problem solving becomes part of the daily practice of every courtroom.

New York offers some hints about the kinds of issues the next generation of problem-solving courts will address. In recent months, state and city officials have focused a problem-solving lens on a range of new criminal justice problems. They have also begun to apply problem-solving concepts outside of criminal court, testing new strategies in family court and housing court as well. What follows are brief descriptions of some of these new directions.

- *Mental-Health Court.* Launched in 2002, the Brooklyn Mental Health Court handles some of the toughest cases to appear in court; cases involving defendants with serious and persistent mental illness. The model is very similar to a drug court: Felony offenders—with the active agreement of judge, prosecutor, and defense attorney—can choose to enter the mental-health court instead of being incarcerated. Once in the program, they are mandated to receive community-based mental-health treatment and required to appear in court regularly to report on their progress. One of the primary challenges for mental-health courts is the nature of mental illness, which for many is a lifelong affliction—courts cannot say "be cured within twelve months."[2] Moreover, mental-health treatment does not lend itself to simple black-and-white determinations of success. There is no equivalent of a urine test for whether someone is successfully managing their illness. For these and other reasons, the mental-health court must create an individualized treatment plan for each participant. The early results from Brooklyn are encouraging—after the first eighteen months of operation, 80 percent of the court's participants were in compliance with their court mandates and making progress toward graduation.[3]

• *Integrated Domestic Violence Court.* The problems that bring a family into the court system are invariably interrelated. Yet under New York's current court structure, a single family confronting an issue like domestic violence can find itself simultaneously in several different courts at the same time—criminal, family, matrimonial—involving multiple judges, attorneys, and other agencies. Each court learns only a piece of the story: decisions are made without all relevant information, families must make multiple appearances in separate courts, and sometimes cases fall between the cracks. Even more disturbing, there is real potential for judges to issue inconsistent or contradictory orders. In response, the New York court system is testing a novel approach to overlapping cases involving domestic violence. By creating a series of experimental Integrated Domestic Violence Courts across the state, court officials are testing the concept of "one family, one judge," ensuring that a single decision maker handles all of a family's court matters related to domestic violence. In the process, the Integrated Domestic Violence Courts seek to reduce recidivism, improve victims' access to services, reduce court inefficiency, and enhance victim satisfaction with the court process.

• *Gun Court.* Many observers have wondered if problem-solving methods can be applied to serious crime. A new gun court in New York City suggests that the answer is "yes." The primary aim of the gun court is to provide swift and certain justice to offenders who violate gun laws. Like the domestic-violence courts, the gun court does not have a rehabilitative orientation. Still, the project embodies one of the core values of problem solving: using data to target resources. The impetus for the court was the discovery that five Brooklyn precincts account for more than half of all shootings in Brooklyn (and about one quarter of all shootings citywide). The gun court focuses exclusively on felony gun possession cases from these five precincts. A single judge and a specially trained prosecution team staff the court. This ensures consistency. It also ensures that the court has a clear understanding of the context in which gun violence occurs. The hope is that the gun court can stiffen penalties, expedite the length of time it takes a gun case to move through the system, and improve law enforcement's intelligence about gun activity in the target precincts.

- *Operation Spotlight.* In a similar vein, when data revealed that 19 percent of the misdemeanor offenses in New York City were committed by only 6 percent of defendants, city officials moved to create a targeted response. Computer technology identifies repeat offenders at the time of their arrest. They are then arraigned in special courtrooms, where they receive priority treatment from prosecutors, who seek higher penalties from judges in these cases. The evidence suggests that this approach has succeeded in strengthening the criminal justice system's response to chronic recidivists—the number of repeat offenders sentenced to jail increased 47 percent from 2002 to 2003.

- *Probation Violation Court.* In many respects, problem-solving courts seek to respond to the problems not just of courts, but of probation departments as well. In enhancing the links between courts and social-service providers, and strengthening accountability mechanisms for offenders, problem-solving courts are essentially giving probation officers new tools. Perhaps the best example of this is the creation of New York City's pilot Probation Violation Courts. These specialized courtrooms handle cases involving offenders who violate the terms of their probation sentences. The Probation Violation Courts are an effort to reduce the length of time it takes to resolve cases in which a probationer has been re-arrested, has absconded from a treatment program, or has tested positive for drugs. Traditionally, these cases have gotten short shrift from judges, who must deal with voluminous daily calendars and heavy trial schedules involving serious crime. The result is that probation officers typically wait until a probationer has accumulated dozens of violations before bringing the matter to court. The message this sends to the average person on probation is that the system isn't working and that misbehavior will be tolerated. The Probation Violation Courts, which are being piloted in three boroughs, address this problem, improving coordination between the courts and probation and ensuring that probation officers intervene at the first warning signs of trouble in a probationer's life rather than letting problems fester.

- *Family Court/Housing Court.* To date, most of the experimentation in problem-solving justice has taken place within criminal court. In recent months, New York officials have begun to explore how problem-solving methods can be brought to bear on problems in housing court and family court as well. For example, in Harlem the New York City housing court is testing whether judges can promote compliance with court orders in landlord-tenant disputes by requiring litigants to return to court to report on their progress making repairs and paying back rent. The housing court in Harlem is also testing whether it is possible to use data to identify "frequent flyers"—litigants who come back to court repeatedly on new cases—and then target interventions in response (for example, providing tenants who cannot pay their rent because of a drug problem with long-term drug treatment or teaching others about money management). Meanwhile, New York City's family court has launched a number of noteworthy problem-solving experiments. Recognizing that young people placed in state facilities reoffend at an alarming rate (as high as 80 percent, according to some studies), the family court in the Bronx is linking selected offenders to community-based services and using a judge to monitor their performance. And building on the foundation set by New York's drug courts, family court is also attempting to introduce a problem-solving approach—specialized training for judges, improved links to social services, improved access to information about litigants—to child abuse and neglect cases across the city.

- *Reentry.* New York City has also embarked upon a process of rethinking how ex-offenders are reintegrated into communities following incarceration. This has included projects that seek to improve discharge planning and an effort to link former Rikers Island inmates to a jobs program immediately following their release. It has also included efforts to bring some of the lessons of the problem-solving court model—including intensive supervision and links to community-based services—to ex-offenders. The trick, at least in New York, is that parolees are not under the supervision of the courts but rather under that of the state's parole department. Accordingly, this means bringing the idea of problem-solving justice to parole officers and administrative law judges.

In short, New York is currently engaged in an aggressive effort to apply the problem-solving approach to new problems and new settings. This has been made possible in large part by the success of New York's pioneering problem-solving courts over the past decade—and by the success of the individuals who cut their teeth in these projects, many of whom have gone on to occupy positions of power in city and state government.

GOING TO SCALE

The goal of "going to scale" is to spread key problem-solving principles throughout state court systems. According to Robert Boruchowitz, the director of the Washington Defender Association in Seattle.

> [One] way of going to scale would be to apply what we do in problem-solving courts to all criminal-court cases. For instance, if you have a defendant accused of assault who has a drug problem, we should be able to address that issue. If we're truly concerned about treatment, then all courts should be concerned about it. If we can show people the benefits of treating each defendant as a whole person with a history and a future like we do in problem-solving courts, then we could alter the whole criminal justice system.[4]

As anyone who has recently been to a conventional state court can attest, we have a long way to go before we can claim that every court is engaged in problem-solving work, and the obstacles are daunting. Courts are by design the most tradition-oriented of our government institutions. Court systems are also sprawling bureaucracies that do not lend themselves to centralized control. A number of factors—including the fact that many judges are independently elected—stand in the way of any reform idea, no matter how good, spreading quickly and broadly throughout a state court system.

But perhaps the biggest roadblock is the notion, firmly held by many attorneys and judges, that solving problems simply isn't part of their job description. This belief is rooted in an understanding of the role of courts that foregrounds such traditional values as neutrality, independence, and equitable dispute resolution.

The challenge for problem-solving innovators is to be able to make the case that problem solving is not antithetical to these values, that courts can perform their traditional role—weighing the merits of each case, safeguarding the rights of individual citizens, and ensuring that laws are obeyed—while also attempting to address the problems of individuals and communities.

A recent study commissioned by the California court system offers some hope.[5] The study included interviews and focus groups with several dozen judges who had presided over problem-solving courts and subsequently returned to conventional courtrooms. Among other things, they were asked whether it was possible to transfer any of the principles from problem-solving courts to their regular practice. There was general agreement among the judges that taking ideas from problem-solving courts was not only possible but desirable. They highlighted several things that they had learned from their time in problem-solving courts—including the value of a problem-solving mindset, direct interaction with defendants, monitoring offenders' performance in treatment, and reaching out to social-service providers—that were appropriate for mainstream use in not only criminal courts but family courts as well.

As these judges implicitly acknowledge, courts operate in increasingly complex societies and are called upon to solve complicated problems. Problem-solving innovators have recognized this and asked courts to respond accordingly. The operative question in a conventional criminal courtroom is fairly straightforward: guilty or not guilty? Anything outside of this narrow framework is deemed irrelevant, inappropriate, and inadmissible. If problem solving is to take root within our courts, judges must be encouraged to ask an expanded array of questions: How can we improve public safety given the facts of this case? How do we address the harm to victims? What are the underlying problems of each defendant and how can we address them?

These are the questions that have driven judges and attorneys to create the drug courts, community courts, and other problem-solving initiatives described in this book. Going forward, the job of problem-solving advocates is to encourage all judges—through judicial training, through changing the way lawyers are taught in law schools, through public pressure—to ask these questions.

While it might seem far-fetched for every judge in every courtroom to pose such questions on a regular basis, it is worth remembering that a majority of state court judges already feel that they should play a role in achieving such nontraditional goals as reducing addiction and working with community groups. National surveys indicate that the public is supportive of these goals as well.

Will problem solving succeed in moving from the margins of the American legal system into the mainstream? While the obstacles are not insignificant, there is much to be hopeful about. A number of states, including New York, Missouri, Louisiana, Utah, Indiana, and others, have declared their intention to build on the lessons of drug courts to test new statewide approaches to addiction, whether through ballot initiative, legislative reform, or change within the judicial branch. Key legislative, executive, and judicial leaders (from both parties) in these states are recognizing that the methods and strategies employed by problem-solving courts are worth investing in over the long haul.

Problem-solving courts are not a magical elixir that will cure all that ails our justice system, and more research and reflection about their costs and impacts is certainly warranted. But problem-solving courts do offer a rare beacon of hope within the criminal justice system. Coming off an era when "nothing works" was accepted as a mantra, the problem-solving approach has demonstrated that it is in fact possible to reduce recidivism, improve compliance with court orders, build safer neighborhoods, and improve public trust in justice. For those of us who care about justice, these are results worth pursuing.

Notes

INTRODUCTION

1 See "Painting the Current Picture: A National Report Card on Drug Courts and Other Problem-Solving Court Programs in the United States," by C. West Huddleston III, Karen Freeman-Wilson, and Donna L. Boone, May 2004, vol. 1, no. 1. Published by the National Drug Court Institute, http://www.ndci.org/publications/paintingcurrentpicture.pdf.

2 Ibid.

3 See chapter 6 for a more thorough review of the problem-solving-court research.

4 Judith S. Kaye, "Delivering Justice Today: A Problem-Solving Approach," *Yale Law & Policy Review* 22:127 (2004): 132.

5 It is worth noting that in some states (including New York) the popularity of problem-solving courts has helped state court leaders argue for additional resources from the political branches.

6 For a more detailed discussion of cost/benefit analyses and problem-solving courts, see chapter 6.

CHAPTER 1

1 Taken from a speech delivered in London, England, on July 7, 2003, at a conference organized by the Home Office.

2   Two caveats are important here. The first is the distinction between state courts and federal courts. The argument presented in this chapter is based on an analysis of state courts, which handle more than nine out of ten criminal cases in the United States. Although in recent years there has been a movement to handle more and more local cases in federal court to take advantage of stiffer penalties and the resources of federal prosecutors, federal courts still have jurisdiction over comparatively few cases. For instance, in 1998, state courts convicted 927,717 adults of a felony, while federal courts convicted 50,494, which means that state courts accounted for 95 percent of the national total. [See U.S. Department of Justice, *Bureau of Justice Statistics, Felony Sentences in State Courts, 1998* (October 2001): 1. In addition to the state/federal distinction, it is also important to note that our focus here is primarily on frontline criminal courts as opposed to other kinds of state courts (e.g., civil court, housing court, juvenile court, matrimonial court, and appellate court).

3   U.S. Department of Justice, Bureau of Justice Statistics, *Felony Sentences in State Courts, 1998* (October 2001): 1. Of course, not every guilty plea is obtained through plea bargaining, but research suggests that most guilty pleas are, in fact, arrived at through some form of negotiation. See Douglas D. Guidorizzi, *"Should We Really "Ban" Plea Bargaining?: The Core Concerns of Plea Bargaining Critics," Emory Law Journal* 47, no. 2 (1999): 753.

4   Jeff Palmer, "Abolishing Plea Bargaining: An End to the Same Old Song and Dance," *American Journal of Criminal Law* 26 (Summer 1999): 510. See also Douglas D. Guidorizzi (note 3) who found evidence of plea bargaining in the nineteenth century: "In New York, for example, statistics from 1839 showed twenty-five percent of convictions resulted from guilty pleas. Ten years later, the rate of guilty pleas climbed to forty-five percent. By 1869, they had jumped to seventy percent, and guilty plea rates

continued to rise each decade until they leveled off around ninety percent in the 1920s. This increase in guilty plea rates clearly suggests an increase in the use of plea bargaining to dispose of criminal cases."

5   Indeed, it can be argued that problem-solving courts represent a move to restore the judicial discretion that over the past generation has been lost to legislative and executive branch policies.

6   Gerard E. Lynch, "Our Administrative System of Criminal Justice," *Fordham Law Review* 2117, 66 (May 1998): 2120 and 2125.

7   *Los Angeles Times*, August 11, 1974.

8   Jeff Palmer, "Abolishing Plea Bargaining: An End to the Same Old Song and Dance," *Am. J. Crim. L.* 26 (Summer 1999): 512, citing Warren E. Burger, "The State of the Judiciary—1970," *American Bar Association Journal* 56 (1970): 929, 931.

9   Anne-Marie Cusac, "What's the Alternative?" *Mother Jones. com*, July 10, 2001, http://motherjones.com news/special_ reports/prisons/alternatives.html.

10   At the end of 2000, the U.S. Bureau of Justice Statistics reported that there were more than 3.8 million people on probation in the United States, making it by far the most common sanction for criminal offenders.

11   Robin Campbell and Robert Victor Wolf, "Problem-Solving Probation: An Overview of Four Community-Based Experiments," *Perspectives* 26, no. 1 (Winter 2002): 28.

12   Ibid.

13   National Center for State Courts, *Child Protective Orders: The Benefits and Limitation for Victims of Domestic Violence* (Williamsburg, VA: The National Center for State Courts, 1997).

14   Office of Justice Programs, Drug Court Clearinghouse and Technical Assistance Project, *Looking at a Decade of Drug Courts* (Washington, DC: American University, 1999).

15   Judith S. Kaye, "Making the Case for Hands-On Courts," *Newsweek*, October 11, 1999, 13.

16 David Rottman, "Does Effective Therapeutic Jurisprudence Require Specialized Courts (and Do Specialized Courts Imply Specialist Judges)?" *Court Review*, Spring 2000, 25.

17 Greg Rohde, "Crackdown on Minor Offenses Swamps New York City Courts," *New York Times*, February 2, 1999.

18 National Institute of Justice, ADAM 1997 Annual Reports on Adult and Juvenile Arrestees (1998), available at http://www.ncjurs.org/nij/textrev.pdf.

19 Greg Berman, "What Is a Traditional Judge Anyway?: Problem-solving in the State Courts," *Judicature* 84, no. 2 (2000): 80.

20 Ibid., 81.

21 Ibid., 80.

22 Mary Wisniewski, "Courts get a fix on drug treatment alternatives in low-level drug cases," *Chicago Lawyer*, June 1999, 6.

23 David Rohde, "Drug Arrests Overloading Court System," *New York Times*, February 17, 2000, B5.

24 Quoted in an interview at http://www.communityjustice.org/frameset.asp?heading=spotlight&heading2=Best+Practices_1&value=Scott+C%2E+Newman%2C+Community+Prosecution+Program%2C+Indianapolis%2C+Indiana+%5F543.

25 John Feinblatt and Derek Denckla, "Prosecutors, defenders and problem-solving courts," *Judicature* 84, no. 4 (January–February 2001): 209.

26 Steve Berry, "Public Shows Little Confidence in Courts," *Los Angeles Times*, November 19, 1998, B1.

27 David B. Rottman and Alan J. Tomkins, "Public Trust and Confidence in the Courts: What Public Opinion Surveys Mean to Judges," *Court Review*, Fall 1999, 24–31.

28 Frances Kahn Zemans, "In the Eye of the Beholder: The Relationship Between the Public and the Courts," in *Courts and Justice: A Reader*, 2nd ed., ed. G. Larry Mays and Peter R. Gregware, (Prospect Heights, IL: Waveland Press, 2000), 15.

29 Quoted in Steve Leben, "Public Trust and Confidence in the Courts," *Court Review*, Fall 1999, 4.

30 "Critical Issues Affecting Public Trust and Confidence in the Courts: A Panel Discussion," *Court Review*, Fall 1999, 56.

31 Greg Berman, "What Is a Traditional Judge Anyway?: Problem solving in the State Courts," *Judicature* 84, no. 2 (September–October 2000): 83.

CHAPTER 2

1 Judith S. Kaye, interview with Robert V. Wolf, September 28, 2001.

2 In a *New York Times* Op-ed, federal judge Donald Lay called for federal courts to adopt the drug-court approach. Donald P. Lay, "Rehab Justice," *New York Times,* November 18, 2004, A31.

3 The role of former Attorney General Janet Reno is worth highlighting. Prior to joining the Justice Department, when she was still a local prosecutor, Reno had helped to create the country's first drug court in Miami, Florida. As Attorney General, Reno used her bully pulpit and her control of federal criminal justice funding sources to encourage other states to follow Florida's example and invest in problem-solving justice.

4 These are the most directly relevant precursors of problem-solving courts, but there are others. Echoes and intellectual underpinnings of problem-solving courts can also be found in the pragmatism and multidisciplinarity of the "law and economics" field (see the writings of Richard Posner); the efforts within many law schools to broaden the definition of good lawyering to include problem solving (see the writings of Paul Brest and Carrie Menkel-Meadow); and the emphasis on decentralization and grassroots creativity of "democratic experimentalism" (see the writings of Michael Dorf and Charles Sabel).

5 J. Kelley, "Divorce Mediation in California," quoted in Daniel McGillis, *Community Mediation Programs: Developments and Challenges*

(Washington, DC: National Institute of Justice, U.S. Department of Justice, 1997), 105.

6   McGillis, *Community Mediation Programs*, 83.

7   Roger Fisher of Harvard Law School, quoted in McGillis, *Community Mediation Programs*, 163.

8   Many have deep reservations about the connections that do exist between these programs and the courts: "The present state of relations between community mediation and the justice system raises a number of concerns. . . . (1) the dependence for funding upon the favor/support of the justice system, (2) the loss of autonomy to turn back inappropriate court referrals, (3) the potential for coerced participation in mediation, (4) the potential to be found at fault is faced by only one party, (5) the misunderstanding of the legal status or basis of mediation processes and outcomes, and (6) the loss of focus on 'community' in community mediation." Timothy Hedeen and Patrick G. Coy, "Community Mediation and the Court System: The Ties That Bind," *Mediation Quarterly*, no. 4.

9   For a short history of the victims' movement, see Marlene Young, "The Victims' Movement: A Confluence of Forces," National Organization for Victim Assistance, speech delivered on February 10, 1997; and Steven D. Walker, "History of the Victims' Movement in the United States," available at http://www.employees.csbsju.edu/jmakepeace/Perspectives2k/fo4Walker.jmm.html.

10 Mark S. Umbreit, *What Is Restorative Justice?* (St. Paul, MN: Center for Restorative Justice & Peacemaking, University of Minnesota, 1999).

11 "Restorative Justice: An Interview with Visiting Fellow Thomas Quinn," *National Institute of Justice Journal*, March 1998, 10–16.

12 Leena Kurki, "Incorporating Restorative and Community Justice into American Sentencing and Corrections," *Sentencing and Corrections Issues for the 21st Century* (Washington, DC: U.S. Department of Justice, September 1999).

13 "Restorative Justice, " *National Institute of Justice Journal*.

14 Ted Gest, *Crime & Politics: Big Government's Erratic Campaign for Law and Order* (Oxford: Oxford University Press, 2001), 160.

15 Herman Goldstein, *Problem-Oriented Policing* (New York: McGraw-Hill, 1990), 33.

16 Ibid., 36.

17 See Michael S. Scott, *Problem-Oriented Policing: Reflections on the First 20 Years* (Washington DC: Office of Community Oriented Policing Services, U.S. Department of Justice, 2000).

18 See James Q. Wilson and George L. Kelling, "Broken Windows: The Police and Neighborhood Safety," *The Atlantic Monthly* 249, no. 3, March 1982, 29–38.

19 Scott, *Problem-Oriented Policing*, iv.

20 Ibid.

21 David B. Wexler and Bruce J. Winick, eds., *Law in a Therapeutic Key: Developments in Therapeutic Jurisprudence* (Durham: Carolina Academic Press, 1996), xvii.

22 Christopher Slobogin, "Therapeutic Jurisprudence: Five Dilemmas to Ponder," in ed. David B. Wexler and Bruce J. Winick, *Law in a Therapeutic Key: Developments in Therapeutic Jurisprudence* (Durham: Carolina Academic Press, 1996), 769.

23 David Rottman and Pamela Casey, "Therapeutic Jurisprudence and the Emergence of Problem-Solving Courts," *National Institute of Justice Journal*, July 1999, 15.

24 Peggy Fulton Hora, William G. Schma, and John T.A. Rosenthal, "Therapeutic Jurisprudence and the Drug Treatment Court Movement: Revolutionizing the Criminal Justice System's Response to Drug Abuse and Crime in America," *Notre Dame Law Review* 74, no. 2 (January 1999), 439–537.

25 David J. Rothman, *Conscience and Convenience: The Asylum and Its Alternatives in Progressive America* (Addison-Wesley Educational Publishers, 1980), 215.

26 Shay Bilchick, *Juvenile Justice: A Century of Change* (Washington DC: U.S. Department of Justice, 1999).

27 There are those who would say that juvenile courts were never terribly benevolent in the first place, arguing that for all of their rhetoric about aiding children, juvenile courts were really a mechanism of social control for managing the behavior of poor and immigrant families.

28 Rothman, *Conscience and Convenience*, 218.

29 Ibid., p. 222–223.

CHAPTER 3

1 Greg Berman, "What Is a Traditional Judge Anyway?: Problem Solving in the State Courts," *Judicature* 84, no. 2 (September–October 2000): 80.

2 Emily Wax, "Hooker Haven No More," *Manhattan Spirit* 13, no. 21, May 23, 1997.

3 Ibid.

4 Robert R. Weidner, *I Won't Do Manhattan: Causes and Consequences of a Decline in Street Prostitution* (2000), 3–4. On file with the author.

5 Robert Victor Wolf, "New Strategies for an Old Profession: A Court and a Community Combat a Streetwalking Epidemic," *Justice System Journal* 22, no. 3, (2001): 349–350.

6 Wax, "Hooker Haven No More."

7 Wolf, "New Strategies for an Old Profession: A Court and a Community Combat a Streetwalking Epidemic," 355.

8 Ibid.

9 Michele Sviridoff, David Rottman, Brian Ostrom, and Richard Curtis, *Dispensing Justice Locally: The Implementation and Effects of the Midtown Community Court* (Amsterdam, The Netherlands: Harwood Academic Publishers, 2000).

10 Ibid., 107.

11 Michael D. Schrunk and Judith N. Phelan, "Problem-Solving Courts: Impact at the Local Level," *Judges Journal*, Winter 2002, 17–20.

12 Interview with John Roman, Urban Institute, September 2002.

13 November 25, 2002, email communication from Robyn Gregory, Office of Multnomah County District Attorney.

14 Interview with Kings County District Attorney Charles J. Hynes, "First Person: Ask the Experts," http://www.community justice.org.

15 Ibid.

16 "Voice from the Neighborhood," *Community Court Reporter*, Portland Oregon Community Court, June 2001.

17 Ibid.

18 Sam Oliver, "Yard Work Program Sows the Seeds of Good Neighborhoods," *Community Court Reporter*, July 2001.

19 *Community Court Reporter*, Portland, Oregon, March 2002.

20 Note that prior to the advent of problem-solving courts, most courts did not see it as being part of their role to monitor compliance. In the past, links to social-service provisions were typically structured as diversion programs. After making a referral, courts stepped aside and let others provide and monitor services. In part, problem-solving courts are a response to the perceived failings of this approach.

21 Sviridoff et al., *Dispensing Justice Locally.*

CHAPTER 4

1 Special thanks to Robert V. Wolf for his work on earlier versions of this chapter. This chapter was developed under grant number SJI-C-01-045 from the State Justice Institute. The points of view expressed are those of the authors and do not necessarily represent the official position or policies of the State Justice Institute.

2 Greg Berman, "What Is a Traditional Judge Anyway?: Problem Solving in the State Courts," *Judicature* 84, no. 2: 82.

3 "Judicial Roundtable: Reflections of Problem-Court Justices," *New York State Bar Journal*, June 2000, 14.

4 It wasn't until the end of the nineteenth century that three

states (Maryland, Delaware, and Oregon) outlawed wife beating—and then it took more than a half century more for domestic violence to enter the nation's consciousness as a serious social problem. See Betsy Tsai, "The Trend Toward Specialized Domestic Violence Courts: Improvements on an Effective Innovation," *Fordham Law Review* 68 (March 2000), 1285.

5 Tsai, "The Trend Toward Specialized Domestic Violence Courts," 1292.

6 Emily Sack, phone interview by Robert V. Wolf, November 29, 2001.

7 Susan Keilitz, "Specialization of Domestic Violence Case Management in the Courts: A National Survey," National Center for State Courts (2000), 3.

8 Ibid., p. 3–4.

9 Dag MacLeod and Julia F. Weber, "Domestic Violence Courts: A Descriptive Study," Judicial Council of California, Administrative Office of the Courts (May 2000), 3.

10 Dierdre Bialo-Padin, chief of the Brooklyn District Attorney's domestic-violence bureau, interview by Robert V. Wolf, November 29, 2001.

11 John Leventhal, interview by Robert V. Wolf, December 6, 2002.

12 Keilitz, "Specialization of Domestic Violence Case Management," 4.

13 Judith S. Kaye, "Lawyering for a New Age," Fordham University Law School, Sonnett Lecture, April 8, 1998.

14 "An Interview with Thomas Zlaket," *Court Review,* Fall 2000, 11.

15 Raymond Norko, phone interview by Anne Gulick.

16 Mark Curriden, "Drug Courts Gain Popularity: Studies show rearrests lower for defendants treated for addiction," *ABA Journal* (May 1994).

17 Berman, ed., "What Is a Traditional Judge Anyway?, 82.

18 Morris B. Hoffman, "The Drug Court Scandal," *North Carolina Law Review* 78 (June 2000): 1479.

19 Berman, ed., "What Is a Traditional Judge Anyway?," 82.

20 Ibid.

21 Patricia Young, phone interview by Nicole Campbell, July 3, 2001.

22 Raymond Norko, phone interview by Anne Gulick.

23 "Judicial Roundtable: Reflections of Problem-Court Justices," *New York State Bar Journal*, June 2000, 14.

24 Stephen V. Manley, interview by Robert V. Wolf, October 2, 2001.

25 William D. McColl, "Baltimore City's Drug Treatment Court: Theory and Practice in an Emerging Field," Maryland Law Review 55 (1996): 517.

26 Laura Ward, interview by Robert V. Wolf, April 10, 2002.

27 "Judicial Roundtable: Reflections of Problem-Court Justices," *New York State Bar Journal*, June 2000, 14.

28 Steven M. Zeidman, in panel titled "The Changing Face of Justice: The Evolution of Problem Solving," at symposium "Problem-Solving Courts: From Adversarial Litigation to Innovative Jurisprudence," *Fordham Urban Law Journal* 29 (June 2002): 1908–9.

29 John Stuart, "Problem Solving Courts: Public Defender's View," *The Judges' Journal*, Winter 2002, 21.

30 Morris B. Hoffman, "The Drug Court Scandal," *North Carolina Law Review* 78 (June 2000): 1479.

31 Morris B. Hoffman, "Therapeutic Jurisprudence, Neo-rehabilitation and the New Judicial Collectivism: The Least Dangerous Branch Becomes the Most Dangerous," *Fordham Urban Law Journal* 29 (June 2002): 2063–2098.

32 Juanita Bing-Newton, "The Changing Face of Justice: What Does the Future Hold for Drug Courts?," *Fordham Urban Law Journal* 29 (June 2002): 1879.

33 Melanie May, phone interview by Anne Gulick.

34 Leslie Leach, interview by Robert V. Wolf, May 9, 2002.

35 Lisa Schreibersdorf, "The Pitfalls of Defenders as 'Team Players,' " *Indigent Defense* (November/December 1997).

36 Scott Wallace, " 'A Level of Teamwork Not Often Seen': An

Interview with Judge Jeffrey S. Tauber," *Indigent Defense* (November/December 1997).

37 Mae C. Quinn, "Whose Team Am I On Anyway?: Musings of a Public Defender About Drug Treatment Court Practice," *New York University Review of Law & Social Change* 26 (2000/2001): 37.

38 Gail Diane Cox, "Drug Courts Do Work," *National Law Journal* (November 23, 1998): A1.

39 Shirley S. Abrahamson, "Courtroom with a View: Building Judicial Independence with Public Participation, *Willamette Journal of International Law & Dispute Resolution* 8 (2000): 13.

40 John Feinblatt and Derek Denckla, eds., "What Does It Mean to Be a Good Lawyer: Prosecutors, Defenders and Problem-Solving Courts," *Judicature* 84, no. 4: 210.

41 Berman, "What Is a Traditional Judge Anyway?," 84.

42 Ibid.

43 Keilitz, "Specialization of Domestic Violence Case Management," 4.

44 Leslie Leach, interview with Robert V. Wolf, May 14, 2002.

45 Ibid.

46 "Judicial Roundtable: Reflections of Problem-Solving Court Justices."

47 William G. Ross, "Extrajudicial Speech: Navigating Perils and Avoiding Pitfalls," *Court Review* (Summer 2001), 38.

48 "Critical Issues Affecting Public Trust and Confidence in the Courts," panel discussion, *Court Review* (Fall 1999), 65.

49 Ibid.

50 "Judicial Roundtable: Reflections of Problem-Court Justices."

51 Berman, ed., "What Is a Traditional Judge Anyway?," 80.

52 Stephen V. Manley, interview with Robert V. Wolf, October 2, 2001.

53 Leslie Leach, interview with Robert V. Wolf, May 14, 2002. In late 2004 Leach was promoted to be an administrative judge in Queens.

54 John Goldkamp, "The Drug Court Response: Issues and Implications for Justice Change," *Albany Law Review* 63 (2000): 926–7.

55 See Michele Sviridoff, David Rottman, Brian Ostrom, and

Richard Curtis, *Dispensing Justice Locally: The Implementation and Effects of the Midtown Community Court* (Amsterdam: Harwood Academic Publishers, 2000; Steven Belenko, "Research on Drug Courts: A Critical Update" (2001) available: http: //www.ndci.org; Lisa Newmark, Mike Rempel, Kelly Diffily, and Kamala Mallik Kane, *Specialized Felony Domestic Violence Courts: Lessons on Implementation and Impacts from the Kings County Experience* (Washington, DC: Urban Institute, 2001).

56 "Judicial Roundtable: Reflections of Problem-Solving Court Justice."

57 Sharon Chatman, phone interview by Nicole Campbell, November 13, 2001.

CHAPTER 5

1 Kim is a pseudonym.

2 "How the Midtown Community Court Changed My Life," *Clinton Chronicle*, October 2000.

3 Crime and Justice Research Institute, *An Honest Chance: Perspectives on Drug Courts*, April 2002.

CHAPTER 6

1 This chapter borrows from Greg Berman and Anne Gulick, "Just the (Unwieldy, Hard to Gather but Nonetheless Essential) Facts, Ma'am: What We Know and Don't Know about Problem-Solving Courts," *Fordham Urban Law Journal* 30, no. 3 (March 2003): 1027–1053. Special thanks to Anne Gulick, Michael Rempel, Michele Sviridoff, Nora Puffett, and Aubrey Fox for their contributions.

2 Quoted in Christian Bourge, "Drug Courts: Viable Alternative to Jail," United Press International, April 2, 2003. Available at: http://www.upi.com/view.cfm?StoryID=20030402-063820-8270r.

3 See Carl Baar and Freda F. Solomon, "The Role of Courts—The Two Faces of Justice," in *The Improvement of the Administration of Justice*,

ed. Gordon M. Griller and E. Keith Stott Jr., Lawyers Conference, Judicial Division, American Bar Association (2002), 16.

4   Robert Martinson, "What Works? Questions and Answers About Prison Reform," *The Public Interest*, no. 35 (1974): 22–55.

5   http://www.ncjrs.org/works/wholedoc.htm

6   Michael Rempel et al., *The New York State Adult Drug Court Evaluation: Policies, Participants and Impacts*, report submitted to the New York State Unified Court System and the U.S. Bureau of Justice Assistance, October 2003.

7   Denise C. Gottfredson et al., "Effectiveness of Drug Treatment Courts: Evidence from a Randomized Trial." Presentation at the Annual Meeting of the American Society of Criminology, November 2002.

8   D. Wilson, O. Mitchell, and D. L. MacKenzie, "A Systematic Review of Drug Court Effects on Recidivism." Paper presented at the Annual Meeting of the American Society of Criminology, Chicago, IL, 2002.

9   Steven Belenko, "Research on Drug Courts: A Critical Review," *National Drug Court Institute Review* 10, no. 29 (1998): 13.

10 B. F. Lewis and R. Ross, "Retention in Therapeutic Communities: Challenges for the Nineties," in *Therapeutic Community: Advances in Research and Application*, ed. F. M. Tims, G. DeLeon, and N. Jainchil (Rockville, MD: NIDA, 1994).

11 S. Holland, "Gateway Houses: Effectiveness of Treatment on Criminal Behavior," *International Journal of Addictions* 13 (1978), 369–381.

12 It is worth noting, however, that the New York drug-court study tells a different story. There, only participants who were able to make it to graduation had lower recidivism rates than the comparison group; there were no discernible effects on those who participated but ultimately failed out of treatment.

13 Adele Harrell, Shannon Cavanagh, and John Roman, *Findings from the Evaluation of the D.C. Superior Court Drug Intervention Program* (Washington, DC: Urban Institute, 1998).

14 Adele Harrell and John Roman, "Reducing Drug Use and Crime Among Offenders: The Impact of Graduated Sanctions," *Journal of Drug Issues* 31, no. 1 (2001).

15 Belenko, "Research on Drug Courts: A Critical Review," 16.

16 Steve Aos et al., *The Comparative Costs and Benefits of Programs to Reduce Crime, Version 4.0* (Olympia, WA: Washington State Institute for Public Policy, 2001).

17 Drug Court Program Office, Department of Justice, *Fiscal Year 2002 Program*, 8.

18 Michael Rempel et al., *The New York State Adult Drug Court Evaluation: Policies, Participants and Impacts*, report submitted to the New York State Unified Court System and the U.S. Bureau of Justice Assistance, October 2003.

19 http://www.ojp.usdoj.gov/aag/messages/drugcourts052003.htm

20 Lisa Newmark et al., *Specialized Felony Domestic Violence Courts: Lessons on Implementation and Impacts from the Kings County Experience* (Urban Institute, 2001).

21 Adele Harrell, "Domestic Violence Courts: Lessons from the National Evaluation of the Judicial Oversight Demonstration." Presentation at the National Association for Court Management, July 17, 2003.

22 Recent research estimates that nearly 80 percent of domestic-violence offenders receiving court mandates are ordered to batterer programs as part of their sanction. In some cases, as in Florida, state law requires program participation of all domestic-violence defendants. See Kerry Healey et al., *Batterer Intervention: Program Approaches and Criminal Justice Strategies*, 1998. Available at http://www.ncjrs.org.

23 Larry W. Bennett and Oliver J. Williams, *Controversies and Recent Studies of Batterer Intervention Program Effectiveness*, 2001, 2. Available at: http://www.vawnet.org/VNL/library/general/AR_bip.html.

24 Robert C. Davis et al., *Does Batterer Treatment Reduce Violence? A Randomized Experiment in Brooklyn*, National Institute of Justice, Jan. 2000.

25 Wayne L. Peterson, presiding judge, and Stephen Thumberg, executive officer, *Evaluation Report for the San Diego County Domestic Violence Courts*, State Justice Institute, 2000.

26 Robert C. Davis et al., *Prosecuting Domestic Violence Cases with Reluctant Victims: Assessing Two Novel Approaches in Milwaukee 1997.* Information taken from abstract in *Legal Interventions in Family Violence: Research Findings and Policy Implications*, July 1998, NCJ.

27 Myrna Dawson and Ronit Donovitzer, "Victim Cooperation and the Prosecution of Domestic Violence in a Specialized Court," *Justice Quarterly* (2001), 593–622.

28 David A. Ford and Mary Jean Regoli, *The Indianapolis Domestic Violence Prosecution Experiment* (1993), Final Report, Indiana University.

29 Christopher D. Maxwell et al., *The Effects of Arrest on Intimate Partner Violence: New Evidence from the Spouse Assault Replication Program, NIJ Research in Brief*, June 2001.

30 Michele Sviridoff, David B. Rottman, Brian Ostrom, and Richard Curtis, *Dispensing Justice Locally: The Implementation and Effects of Midtown Community Court* (Amsterdam: Harwood Academic Publishers, 2000).

31 Ibid., 135.

32 Ibid.

33 Ibid.

34 Ibid., 136.

35 Ibid., 155.

36 Michele Sviridoff et al., *Dispensing Justice Locally: The Impacts, Cost and Benefits of the Midtown Community Court* (2002). Unpublished. National Institute of Justice, U.S. Department of Justice.

37 Ibid.

38 Community Court Project Outcomes and Savings, February 2002, Multnomah County District Attorney.

39 Sviridoff et al., 9–15.

40 David B. Rottman and Randall M. Hansen, *How Recent Court Users*

View the State Courts: Perceptions of African-American, Latinos and Whites (2001). Available at http://www.ncsc.dni.us/RESEARCH/ RecentCourtsPaper.pdf.

41 Unpublished; on file with the Center for Court Innovation.

42 Ibid.

43 Leslie Paik, *Surveying Communities: A Guide for Community Justice Planners* (Washington, D.C.: Bureau for Justice Assistance, 2003).

44 Ibid.

CHAPTER 7

1 This chapter borrows from John Feinblatt, Greg Berman, and Derek Denckla, "Judicial Innovation at the Crossroads: The Future of Problem-Solving Courts," *The Court Manager* 15, no. 3 (2000): 28–33; and John Feinblatt, Greg Berman, and Michele Sviridoff, "Neighborhood Justice at the Midtown Community Court," *Crime and Place, Plenary Papers of the 1997 Conference on Criminal Justice Research and Evaluation* (1998). http://www.ncjrs. org/txtfiles/168618.txt. Many thanks to Michele Sviridoff and Derek Denckla for their contributions.

2 Greg Berman, "What Is a Traditional Judge Anyway: Problem Solving in the State Courts," *Judicature* 84, no. 2 (September–October 2000): 84.

3 Morris Hoffman, "The Drug Court Scandal," *North Carolina Law Review* 78 (2000): 1437–1534.

4 Anthony C. Thompson, "Courting Disorder: Some Thoughts on Community Courts," *Washington University Journal of Law and Policy* 10 (2002): 67.

5 Ibid., 85.

6 Freda F. Solomon, "The Impact of Quality-of-Life Policing on Arrest and Arrestee Characteristics in New York City." Paper prepared for the Annual Meeting of the American Society of Criminology, November 13, 2002.

7 See Feinblatt, Berman, and Sviridoff, "Neighborhood Justice at

the Midtown Community Court."

8   Michele Sviridoff et al., *Dispensing Justice Locally: The Impacts, Costs and Benefits of the Midtown Community Court* (2002), Executive Summary, 3.

9   See chapter 2 for a detailed discussion of the similarities and differences between juvenile courts and problem-solving courts.

10 Eleventh Annual Symposium on Contemporary Urban Challenges, Problem-Solving Courts: From Adversarial Litigation to Innovative Jurisprudence, "What the Data Shows," *Fordham Urban Law Journal* 29 (June 2002): 1833.

11 James L. Nolan Jr., *Reinventing Justice: The American Drug Court Movement* (Princeton: Princeton University Press, 2001), 204.

12 Interview with Cait Clarke, November 17, 2004.

13 Denise C. Gottfredson et al., "Effectiveness of Drug Treatment Courts: Evidence from a Randomized Trial." Paper prepared for the Annual Meeting of the American Society of Criminology, November 2002.

14 Adele Harrell, "Judging Drug Courts: Balancing the Evidence," *Criminology and Public Policy* (forthcoming).

15 Ibid.

16 John Feinblatt and Derek Denckla, "Prosecutors, Defenders and Problem-solving Courts," *Judicature* (January–February 2001): 207–214.

17 Michele Sviridoff et al., *Dispensing Justice Locally: The Implementation and Effects of the Midtown Community Court* (Amsterdam: Harwood Academic Publishers, 2000).

18 Ibid., 210.

19 Feinblatt and Denckla, 211.

20 Of course, any effort to institutionalize these kinds of structural changes must pay careful attention to balancing the rights of defendants (and the demands of defenders) with the rights of victims (and the imperatives of prosecutors).

21 While we focus here primarily on defender concerns, it is

important to acknowledge that prosecutors have their own issues with problem-solving courts, including concerns about the appropriateness of treatment as an alternative to incarceration for many offenders.

22 Feinblatt and Denckla, 210.

23 John S. Goldkamp, "The Drug Court Response: Issues and Implications for Justice Change," *Albany Law Review* (2000): 923, 952.

24 See comments of Susan Hendricks, panel titled "The Impact of Problem Solving on the Lawyer's Role and Ethics," *Fordham Law Journal,* 29 (June 2002): 1920–1921.

25 Daniel L. Greenberg, "Prosecutors Are the Wrong Gatekeepers," *New York Law Journal,* letter to the editor, March 17, 2003.

26 The same can be said about other problem-solving models, like gun courts and probation-violation courts, where the court's focus is on improving the accountability of offenders.

27 Bennett H. Brummer, "Criminal Law Symposium: Independence, Professional Judgment: The Essence of Freedom," *St. Thomas Law Review* 10 (Spring 1998): 607.

28 Lisa Newmark et al., *Specialized Felony Domestic Violence Courts: Lessons on Implementation and Impacts from the Kings County Experience* (Washington, D.C.: Urban Institute, October 2001), 45.

29 Interview with Sarah Glazer.

30 Conversation with Greg Berman, November 15, 2004.

31 John Stuart, "Problem-Solving Courts: A Public Defender's Perspective," *ABA Judges Journal* 41, no. 1 (Winter 2002): 24.

32 Eric Lane, "Due Process and Problem-Solving Courts," *Fordham Urban Law Journal* 30, no. 3 (March 2003): 958.

CONCLUSION

1 Henry Ruth and Kevin R. Reitz, *The Challenge of Crime: Rethinking Our Response* (Cambridge: Harvard University Press, 2003).

2 John Goldkamp and Cheryl Irons-Guynn, *Judicial Strategies for*

the Mentally Ill in the Criminal Caseload: Mental Health Courts in Fort Lauderdale, Seattle, San Bernadino, and Anchorage (Washington, DC: U.S. Department of Justice, 2000).

3   Carol Fisler, "Building Trust and Managing Risk: A Look at a Felony Mental Health Court," unpublished paper on file with author.

4   John Feinblatt and Derek Denckla, "Prosecutors, Defenders and Problem-Solving Courts," *Judicature* 84, no. 4 (January–February 2001): 214.

5   D. Farole, N. Puffett, M. Rempel, and F. Bryne. *Collaborative Justice in Conventional Courts: Opportunities and Barriers*. Report submitted to the California Administrative Office of the Courts, Center for Court Innovation, 2004.

Index

Problem-oriented policing, 46–49
  components of, 47
  Herman Goldstein on, 46–47
Problem-solving courts, 4–13,
    31–58
  accountability of, 108–9
  alternate dispute resolution
    in, 39–42
  appropriateness of, 105–6
  benefits of, 10–11
  challenges for, 196
  cost savings from, 13
  countries with, 10
  criticisms of, 10
  diversity of, 32
  elements of, 5–7
  example of, 8–9
  funding of, 32
  future of, 189–98
  goal of, 32
  and juvenile court, 52–58
  Judith S. Kaye on, 12
  Scott Newman on goals of, 35
  number of, 32
  origins of, 38–39
  principles of, 34–38
  principles of, for traditional
    courts, 196–97
  and problem-oriented
    policing, 46–49
  public support for goals of, 197
  research about, 129
  results of, 11

scope of, 33
shoplifting example of, 33–34
and therapeutic jurispru-
    dence, 49–52
types of, 7–8
and victims' movement, 43–46
Progressive Movement, 52
Property owners, 75
Proportionality, 175–78
Prosecutors:
  changing role of, 86, 181
  community courts supported
    by, 71
  and ex parte communication,
    118–19
  local, 71–72
  and neighborhood meetings, 85
  and team approach, 115, 116
Prostitution, 93–94
  effects of, 68–70
  Barbara Feldt on, 62
  and health education, 93
  insurmountable problems, 105
  Kim's story about, 131–37
  in Midtown Manhattan, 60–66
  and "time served" sentences, 175
  volume of arrests for, 165
Prostitution enforcement, 61–62
Prostitution intervention, 64–65
Public admonition, 70
Public defenders:
  Lee H. Carson on frustration
    of, 26